JIM EINSTEIN

THE VALUE CREATOR

Driving Revenue and Impact in Business

Contents

Introduction: Unleashing the Power of the Value Creator

In the vast expanse of the business landscape, there exists a rare breed of visionaries, leaders, and innovators who possess a unique and awe-inspiring ability to transcend the ordinary, to unleash the boundless power of creation, and to transform the very fabric of the industries they touch. These exceptional individuals are not just leaders; they are alchemists of prosperity, sculptors of success, and architects of impact. They are the Value Creators.

Welcome to a journey of discovery, inspiration, and empowerment – "THE VALUE CREATOR: Driving Revenue and Impact in Business." In these pages, we shall unravel the secrets of these extraordinary individuals who, like guiding stars in the night sky, navigate businesses and organizations towards greatness. They possess an innate ability to weave dreams into reality, turning challenges into stepping stones, and instilling a sense of purpose in the hearts of all who follow them.

What defines the essence of a Value Creator? They are the visionaries who see potential where others see obstacles. The audacious trailblazers who shatter limitations and redefine possibilities. The catalysts who spark innovation and embrace change as a springboard to unprecedented growth. A Value Creator's journey is not for the faint-hearted; it requires a resolute commitment to excellence, a relentless pursuit of impact, and an unwavering belief in the transformative power of their endeavors.

In the chapters that follow, we shall delve deep into the realms of greatness, exploring the stories of legendary Value Creators whose names echo through time. Through their narratives, we shall uncover the core principles that set them apart: their unwavering dedication to value, the finesse with which they steer revenues, and the profound impact they leave on businesses, organizations, and society as a whole.

Beyond the history that inspires us, we shall journey into the present, where the ripple effects of contemporary Value Creators reverberate across diverse industries. Their tales of disruption and innovation will ignite a spark within you, urging you to unleash your inner Value Creator – to embrace the untapped potential that lies dormant, waiting for the catalyst of change.

This book is not merely an ode to greatness; it is a guidebook for transformation. It is a call to action for every individual, in every position, in every organization, to awaken the value creator within. Through strategic insights, real-life case studies, and data-backed analyses, you shall find the tools to nurture a value-centric mindset, unleash your creativity, and propel your business towards exponential growth.

Prepare to embark on a journey that transcends geographical boundaries, resonates with diverse cultures, and touches the hearts of a global audience. *"THE VALUE CREATOR: Driving Revenue and Impact in Business" is not just a book; it is a catalyst for change, a symphony of inspiration, and a map to navigate the uncharted territories of success.*

So, dear readers, fasten your seatbelt, open your mind to the realm of possibilities, and let the adventure begin. As you flip through these pages, may you be captivated, breathless, and motivated to embrace your destiny as a Value Creator – to shape the future, to drive revenue, and to make an indelible impact on the canvas of the business world. The world awaits your unique brilliance; let the journey commence!

1

1

The Essence of a Value Creator

In the realm of business and innovation, the concept of the Value Creator stands as a luminous beacon, guiding organizations towards unrivaled success and transforming mere ventures into powerful forces of impact. This chapter delves deep into the very essence of these remarkable individuals – those visionaries who possess an innate ability to shape destinies and leave an indelible mark on the world.

This chapter is a gateway to understanding the profound meaning and significance of being a Value Creator. We embark on a voyage of self-discovery, exploring the attributes, traits, and characteristics that define these extraordinary individuals. Through compelling narratives and illuminating insights, we reveal the heart of what sets Value Creators apart – their unyielding commitment to adding value in every aspect of their endeavors.

A Value Creator is not just a title or a role; it is a state of mind, a way of being. As we immerse ourselves in their stories, we come to recognize that every person, regardless of their position or background, holds the potential to unleash the Value Creator within. The first chapter serves as an invitation to introspection, urging readers to recognize the untapped reservoir of creativity, innovation, and transformation that resides within each of us.

Moreover, we explore how the essence of a Value Creator transcends mere business realms. It extends to the core of leadership, where driving revenue and creating impact become the primary guiding principles. Through compelling anecdotes and real-world examples, readers will witness how these visionary leaders leave an indelible mark on their organizations, instilling a culture of excellence and empowerment that reverberates across the entire ecosystem.

In the quest to comprehend the essence of a Value Creator, we find not just answers but a map for personal and professional growth. The chapter culminates with a call to action, challenging readers to embrace their potential as Value Creators – to embody the traits of innovation, resilience, and unwavering dedication to value.

Prepare to be captivated by the extraordinary stories of those who have harnessed the power of the Value Creator within. As we embark on this enlightening journey, may the essence of a Value Creator ignite a fire within every reader, motivating them to embrace the path of value-driven success and transformation.

Defining the Value Creator: Who is a Value Creator?

At the heart of every successful business, organization, or endeavor, there exists a guiding force – an individual whose impact transcends conventional boundaries and whose ability to create value sets them apart as a true visionary. This guiding force is none other than the Value Creator – a dynamic, innovative, and transformative figure who shapes destinies and leads businesses towards unparalleled growth and impact.

Defining a Value Creator is not confined to a singular label or role; it is a multifaceted concept that encompasses diverse attributes and characteristics. At its core, a Value Creator is an individual who possesses an unwavering commitment to adding value in every aspect of their endeavors. Whether they are entrepreneurs, executives, leaders, or team members, their mindset revolves around contributing something meaningful and impactful to the world.

One key trait of a Value Creator is their visionary outlook. They possess an innate ability to see potential where others see obstacles, to identify opportunities where others perceive challenges. Their visionary thinking allows them to anticipate trends, spot gaps in the market, and conceptualize innovative solutions that revolutionize industries.

In addition to their foresight, Value Creators exhibit a remarkable entrepreneurial spirit. They have the courage to take risks, the audacity to challenge the status quo, and the resilience to persevere in the face of uncertainty. They are not confined by conventional norms; instead, they embrace disruption as a catalyst for growth and seize opportunities that others may overlook.

At the heart of their endeavors lies a profound dedication to value. Value Creators prioritize the needs of their stakeholders – be it customers, employees, partners, or society at large. They understand that sustainable success is derived from delivering tangible benefits and creating a positive impact on the lives of those they serve.

Furthermore, a Value Creator is an eternal learner, constantly seeking to expand their knowledge, skills, and expertise. They possess an insatiable appetite for learning from their experiences, their peers, and the world around them. This willingness to adapt and grow allows them to stay ahead of the curve, continuously evolving to meet the demands of an ever-changing landscape.

Collaboration is another cornerstone of a Value Creator's approach. They understand that greatness is rarely achieved in isolation, and as such, they foster a culture of teamwork and partnership. By leveraging the strengths of diverse talents, they amplify their impact and create a collaborative ecosystem that fuels growth and innovation.

An essential aspect of a Value Creator's identity is their unshakable integrity. Ethics and honesty form the foundation of their actions, and they hold themselves accountable to the highest standards of conduct. This moral compass not only earns them trust and respect but also reinforces their influence as genuine and authentic leaders.

A Value Creator's impact extends far beyond the financial realm. They are catalysts for social change, advocates for sustainability, and champions of positive transformation. Their endeavors reflect a profound sense of responsibility towards society, and they consistently seek to align their business objectives with the greater good.

In essence, a Value Creator embodies the spirit of a purpose-driven leader. They are not solely focused on personal gain or short-term success. Instead, they are driven by a sense of purpose – a deep-rooted desire to make a lasting, meaningful impact on the world around them.

As we delve deeper into the world of Value Creators in the following chapters, we will encounter inspiring tales of individuals from various fields who have harnessed their innate potential to create value and drive impact. From historic figures to contemporary trailblazers, their stories will serve as guiding beacons, igniting a fire within us to embrace the path of the Value Creator.

In conclusion, a Value Creator is more than just a title or a position – it is a way of being, a mindset, and a transformative force that has the potential to shape destinies, drive revenue, and make an indelible impact on the canvas of the business world. It is an invitation to every individual to recognize their inherent ability to add value and become architects of positive change in the world. The journey of the Value Creator awaits us, and with it, the boundless possibilities of growth, success, and lasting impact.

The Traits and Characteristics of Highly Effective Value Creators

Highly effective Value Creators possess a unique blend of traits and characteristics that set them apart as true visionaries and catalysts for transformation. These qualities enable them to drive revenue, create substantial impact, and leave an indelible mark on the business landscape. In this chapter, we explore the key traits that define these exceptional individuals and contribute to their unparalleled success.

1. *Visionary Thinking:* At the core of every effective Value Creator lies a visionary mindset. They possess the ability to see beyond the present, envisioning possibilities that others may overlook. Their forward-thinking outlook enables them to anticipate industry trends, identify emerging opportunities, and devise innovative solutions that disrupt conventional norms.

2. *Resilience and Grit:* The journey of a Value Creator is not without challenges and setbacks. However, what sets them apart is their resilience and unwavering determination to overcome obstacles. They embrace failures as learning experiences, bouncing back with renewed vigor to achieve their goals.

3. *Courageous Risk-Taking:* Effective Value Creators are not afraid to take calculated risks. They understand that growth and innovation often require stepping into uncharted territory. Their willingness to venture beyond their comfort zones sets them apart as pioneers in their fields.

4. *Passion and Purpose:* Value Creators are driven by a deep sense of purpose and passion for their work. Their endeavors are not solely motivated by financial gain but are guided by a genuine desire to make a positive impact on their stakeholders and society at large.

5. *Adaptability and Continuous Learning:* In a rapidly changing business landscape, adaptability is crucial for success. Highly effective Value Creators embrace change and view it as an opportunity for growth. They are avid learners, continuously seeking knowledge and insights to stay at the forefront of their industries.

6. *Empathy and Customer-Centricity:* Understanding the needs and desires of their customers is a hallmark of a highly effective Value Creator. They place a strong emphasis on empathy, actively listening to their stakeholders, and tailoring their solutions to address their pain points.

7. *Innovative Problem-Solving:* Value Creators thrive on solving complex challenges with innovative solutions. They possess a keen ability to think outside the box, finding creative ways to turn obstacles into opportunities.

8. *Collaborative Leadership:* Effective Value Creators recognize the power of collaboration and foster a culture of teamwork within their organizations. They empower their teams, encourage diverse perspectives, and create an environment where innovation flourishes.

9. *Integrity and Ethical Leadership:* The trust of stakeholders is paramount for a Value Creator. They lead with integrity, adhering to ethical principles, and upholding their commitments. Their authenticity and transparency enhance their credibility and influence.

10. *Long-Term Vision:* While Value Creators may achieve short-term successes, their focus remains on long-term sustainable growth. They understand that enduring impact is achieved through responsible, far-sighted strategies that

benefit all stakeholders.

11. *Data-Driven Decision Making:* In a data-driven world, effective Value Creators rely on insights and analytics to inform their decisions. They leverage data to validate their strategies, identify trends, and optimize performance.

12. *Social and Environmental Responsibility*: Beyond financial success, Value Creators exhibit a deep sense of social and environmental responsibility. They integrate sustainable practices into their business models, contributing to positive societal and environmental outcomes.

As we delve into the lives and stories of highly effective Value Creators, we find that these traits are not exclusive to a select few but can be cultivated and nurtured in individuals from all walks of life. The journey of becoming a Value Creator involves embracing these characteristics, aligning actions with purpose, and persistently striving to add value in every endeavor.

Through the lens of these remarkable individuals, we witness how these traits synergize to create a force that transcends boundaries, drives revenue, and positively impacts businesses and society. It is an invitation to every reader to unlock their potential as a Value Creator – to embrace visionary thinking, resilient determination, and an unwavering commitment to value-driven success. As we continue our exploration, let us be inspired by the remarkable stories of highly effective Value Creators, and may their journey ignite the spark within us to become architects of transformation in the world of business and beyond.

Recognizing the Value Creator in You

Recognizing the Value Creator within ourselves is a profound journey of self-discovery, empowerment, and transformation. It is an exploration of our inherent potential to create value, drive revenue, and make a lasting impact on the world around us. In this chapter, we embark on a quest to understand the key elements that define a Value Creator and how we can awaken these qualities within ourselves.

1. *Embracing Self-Awareness:* The first step in recognizing the Value Creator in you is to cultivate self-awareness. This involves understanding our strengths, weaknesses, passions, and purpose. Self-awareness allows us to identify the unique gifts and talents we possess, which form the foundation of our journey as a Value Creator.

2. *Unleashing Creativity:* Creativity is the lifeblood of a Value Creator. It is the driving force behind innovative solutions, groundbreaking ideas, and transformative endeavors. By embracing creativity, we tap into our ability to see opportunities where others may see challenges and discover new paths to add value in our endeavors.

3. *Nurturing a Growth Mindset:* A growth mindset is essential for unlocking our potential as Value Creators. It involves believing in our ability to learn, adapt, and improve continuously. With a growth mindset, we view failures as stepping stones and setbacks as opportunities for growth, propelling us forward on our journey of value creation.

4. *Cultivating Passion and Purpose:* Recognizing the Value Creator within requires aligning our actions with our passions and purpose. When we find a sense of meaning and fulfillment in our work, we naturally strive to make a positive impact. Embracing our purpose empowers us to channel our efforts towards creating value for others and leaving a legacy that extends beyond our individual pursuits.

5. *Becoming Customer-Centric:* Just as effective Value Creators prioritize the needs of their customers, we too must adopt a customer-centric approach. Understanding the desires, pain points, and aspirations of our stakeholders enables us to tailor our offerings and solutions to deliver maximum value.

6. *Embodying Resilience:* Value Creators face challenges and obstacles on their path to success, but their resilience enables them to persevere. Recognizing the Value Creator in ourselves involves developing the fortitude to bounce back from setbacks and stay committed to our vision, regardless of the hurdles we encounter.

7. *Taking Courageous Action:* To be a Value Creator, we must take action and turn our ideas into reality. Courage is the catalyst that propels us to step outside our comfort zones, embrace calculated risks, and seize opportunities that align with our purpose.

8. *Building Collaborative Networks:* Recognizing the Value Creator within entails building collaborative networks of support. Surrounding ourselves with like-minded individuals, mentors, and allies amplifies our impact and provides a support system to navigate challenges and celebrate successes.

9. *Embracing Continuous Learning:* A Value Creator's journey is a perpetual quest for knowledge and growth. We must embrace a hunger for learning, seek out new experiences, and stay curious about emerging trends and opportunities in our industry.

10. *Championing Integrity:* The bedrock of a Value Creator's influence lies in their integrity and ethical leadership. Recognizing the Value Creator in ourselves means upholding honesty, transparency, and accountability in our actions, earning the trust and respect of those we serve.

11. *Measuring Impact:* As we progress on our path as Value Creators, it is crucial to measure the impact of our efforts. Quantifying the value we

create allows us to understand our contribution, optimize our strategies, and continuously improve our outcomes.

Recognizing the Value Creator within ourselves is a transformative journey that requires introspection, self-belief, and a commitment to adding value. By embracing our creativity, resilience, and purpose, we unlock our potential to drive revenue, make a significant impact, and contribute to positive change in our spheres of influence.

As we embark on this voyage of self-recognition, let us be inspired by the remarkable stories of Value Creators from diverse fields. Their journeys serve as beacons of inspiration, guiding us towards embracing our potential as architects of transformation in the world of business and society. The power to recognize the Value Creator in you lies within; now, let us take the bold step towards unleashing it to shape a brighter, value-driven future.

2

2

The Impact of a Value Creator

In the ever-evolving world of business and innovation, a powerful force emerges – the Impact of the Value Creator. This chapter embarks on a captivating journey to explore the profound effects these visionary individuals have on businesses, organizations, and society as a whole.

The Impact of a Value Creator extends far beyond financial success; it encompasses a transformative influence that shapes industries, revolutionizes practices, and uplifts communities. Through the lens of real-life case studies and illuminating insights, this chapter delves deep into the stories of extraordinary Value Creators across diverse fields.

We shall witness how these remarkable individuals, armed with visionary thinking and an unwavering dedication to value, ignite a ripple effect of positive change. Their endeavors leave an indelible mark, propelling organizations towards unprecedented growth and fostering a culture of innovation that permeates throughout the business landscape.

From historic figures whose legacies continue to shape modern businesses to contemporary trailblazers who drive exponential revenue growth, this chapter sheds light on the strategic approaches employed by Value Creators to navigate challenges and seize opportunities.

Furthermore, we shall explore how the Impact of a Value Creator extends beyond boardrooms and bottom lines. By championing ethical leadership, social responsibility, and sustainable practices, they redefine the purpose of businesses, transcending profit-driven goals to create a lasting impact on society and the environment.

As we unravel the Impact of the Value Creator, we invite readers to draw inspiration from these extraordinary individuals and embrace the potential within themselves to make a difference. The journeys of these visionaries serve as guiding beacons, illuminating the path towards becoming catalysts for positive transformation.

Prepare to be captivated by the stories of remarkable Value Creators whose footprints resonate across time and space. From small enterprises to multinational corporations, their endeavors demonstrate that the Impact of a Value Creator knows no bounds, reaching far and wide to create a more prosperous and sustainable future.

In this chapter, we uncover the secrets behind the lasting impact of these remarkable individuals – their fearless pursuit of innovation, their unyielding commitment to value-driven success, and their unwavering belief in the transformative power of their actions.

So, as we embark on this enlightening exploration, may the stories of these extraordinary Value Creators inspire us to embrace our potential as architects of change and unlock the profound impact that lies dormant within each of us. The journey of the Impact of the Value Creator awaits; let us commence on this transformative path towards driving revenue and creating a lasting legacy of positive transformation.

Case Studies of Extraordinary Value Creators Across Industries

1. Elon Musk - Automotive and Space Exploration:
Elon Musk, the visionary founder of Tesla and SpaceX, stands as a prime example of an extraordinary Value Creator. With Tesla, he disrupted the automotive industry by pioneering electric vehicles with cutting-edge technology and design. Musk's commitment to sustainability and innovation propelled Tesla to become a leading force in the industry, driving widespread adoption of electric vehicles.

Additionally, through SpaceX, Musk revolutionized space exploration by reducing the cost of launching payloads and developing reusable rockets. His audacious vision to colonize Mars and make humanity a multi-planetary species showcases the boundless impact a Value Creator can have on the future of humanity.

2. Indra Nooyi - Consumer Goods:
As the former CEO of PepsiCo, Indra Nooyi demonstrated exceptional leadership and value creation within the consumer goods industry. Under her guidance, PepsiCo diversified its product portfolio, emphasizing healthier options and sustainability initiatives. Her strategic focus on aligning business goals with social responsibility led to the company's significant revenue growth and positive impact on health and sustainability practices within the industry.

3. Jeff Bezos - E-Commerce and Technology:
Jeff Bezos, the founder of Amazon, epitomizes the transformative power of a Value Creator in the world of e-commerce and technology. With a relentless commitment to customer-centricity and continuous innovation, Bezos grew Amazon from a humble online bookstore to the world's largest e-commerce platform and a leader in cloud computing services through Amazon Web Services (AWS).

Bezos' vision of long-term growth and his bold moves into diverse sectors, such as artificial intelligence and space exploration through Blue Origin, demonstrate how a Value Creator's impact can extend far beyond a single industry.

4. *Mary Barra - Automotive Manufacturing:*

As the CEO of General Motors (GM), Mary Barra exemplifies a Value Creator who has brought about significant change in the automotive manufacturing sector. Under her leadership, GM embraced electrification and autonomous vehicle technology, positioning the company as a major player in the future of mobility.

Barra's strategic decisions to focus on customer needs, invest in new technologies, and foster a culture of innovation have revitalized GM's brand and propelled the company into the forefront of the automotive industry's transformation.

5. *Jack Ma - E-commerce and Fintech:*

Jack Ma, the founder of Alibaba Group, redefined e-commerce in China and beyond, showcasing the profound impact a Value Creator can have on a global scale. Through Alibaba's innovative platforms, Ma enabled millions of businesses to thrive in the digital marketplace, driving significant revenue growth and economic empowerment.

Furthermore, Ma's ventures into financial technology through Ant Group demonstrated his visionary approach to addressing the needs of the under-served and revolutionizing the fintech landscape.

These case studies serve as compelling evidence of how extraordinary Value Creators transcend industries, driving substantial revenue growth, and making a lasting impact. By exemplifying traits such as visionary thinking, innovation, customer-centricity, and a commitment to social responsibility, these individuals have left an indelible mark on the business world and society at large.

Their stories inspire us to recognize the Value Creator within ourselves and embrace our potential to drive change, lead with purpose, and create a meaningful impact in the industries and communities we serve. As we draw insights from these exceptional leaders, we embark on a transformative journey to unlock our own potential as architects of positive transformation. The Impact of these Value Creators extends far beyond their individual ventures; it serves as a testament to the boundless possibilities that arise when visionary thinking and purpose-driven action converge.

How Value Creators Revolutionize Businesses and Organizations

Value Creators revolutionize businesses and organizations by infusing them with innovation, purpose, and a relentless commitment to adding value. Through their visionary thinking and strategic approach, they bring about transformative changes that reshape industries and drive sustainable growth. Here are some key ways in which Value Creators revolutionize businesses and organizations:

1. *Visionary Leadership:* Value Creators inspire and lead their teams with a compelling vision for the future. They have a clear sense of purpose and communicate it effectively, aligning the entire organization towards a common goal. Their visionary leadership ignites passion and enthusiasm within the workforce, fostering a culture of innovation and collaboration.

2. *Customer-Centricity:* Value Creators place a strong emphasis on understanding and prioritizing the needs of their customers. They listen to feedback, analyze data, and continuously seek ways to improve the customer experience. By putting customers at the heart of their decision-making, they build loyalty,

trust, and long-term relationships.

3. *Disruptive Innovation:* Value Creators are disruptors who challenge conventional practices and embrace change. They identify gaps in the market, anticipate emerging trends, and introduce innovative solutions that set their organizations apart from competitors. Through continuous innovation, they stay ahead of the curve and drive industry evolution.

4. *Embracing Technology:* Value Creators recognize the transformative power of technology and integrate it strategically into their business operations. They leverage digital tools, data analytics, and artificial intelligence to enhance efficiency, optimize processes, and deliver personalized experiences to customers.

5. *Nurturing a Culture of Excellence:* Value Creators foster a culture of excellence where employees are encouraged to think creatively, take calculated risks, and contribute their unique perspectives. They invest in employee development, recognizing that a motivated and empowered workforce is key to driving organizational success.

6. *Social and Environmental Responsibility:* Value Creators understand the importance of corporate social responsibility and sustainable practices. They integrate ethical considerations into their business strategies, supporting social causes, reducing environmental impact, and building trust with stakeholders.

7. *Agility and Adaptability:* Value Creators equip their organizations with the agility to respond to rapidly changing market conditions. They embrace uncertainty and proactively adapt to new challenges, ensuring that their businesses remain resilient and poised for growth in dynamic environments.

8. *Collaboration and Partnerships:* Value Creators recognize the power of collaboration and actively seek strategic partnerships. By leveraging the

strengths of external entities, they expand their reach, access new markets, and capitalize on complementary expertise.

9. *Data-Driven Decision Making:* Value Creators base their decisions on data and insights rather than intuition alone. They employ advanced analytics to identify patterns, predict trends, and make informed choices that maximize value creation and revenue growth.

10. *Long-Term Vision:* Value Creators think beyond short-term gains and focus on sustainable, long-term success. They invest in research and development, talent acquisition, and infrastructure, ensuring that their organizations are well-positioned for continued growth and impact.

By embodying these principles, Value Creators revolutionize businesses and organizations, elevating them to new heights of success and influence. Their impact extends far beyond financial gains; they inspire positive change, influence industry landscapes, and leave a lasting legacy of value creation for generations to come. As more leaders embrace the mindset of a Value Creator, the potential for transformation and positive impact in the business world becomes boundless.

The Ripple Effect: Impacting Business and Society

In the realm of value creation, the impact of a Value Creator extends far beyond the confines of individual businesses or organizations. Like ripples in a pond, their actions create a profound effect that permeates the entire business landscape and society at large. Chapter 2 of "THE VALUE CREATOR: Driving Revenue and Impact in Business" explores the transformative power of the Ripple Effect – how the actions of extraordinary individuals ripple outwards, shaping industries, inspiring change, and leaving an indelible mark on the world.

1. *Transforming Industries:* The impact of a Value Creator can be felt in industries where they disrupt conventional practices and redefine norms. By introducing groundbreaking innovations and game-changing solutions, Value Creators revolutionize the competitive landscape, driving other players to adapt and raise their standards. Through this transformation, entire industries are pushed to innovate and evolve, raising the bar for excellence and driving collective growth.

2. *Catalyzing Economic Growth:* The Ripple Effect of a Value Creator's impact is not limited to their immediate sphere of influence. As businesses thrive and grow under their visionary leadership, a positive economic impact ripples through the supply chain, generating opportunities for suppliers, vendors, and service providers. The resulting economic growth stimulates job creation, boosts consumer spending, and contributes to the prosperity of communities.

3. *Inspiring Entrepreneurship:* Value Creators serve as beacons of inspiration for aspiring entrepreneurs. Their success stories ignite a spark of possibility in the minds of individuals seeking to make their mark in the business world. By showcasing the rewards of innovation, perseverance, and customer-centricity, Value Creators encourage others to embark on entrepreneurial journeys, further enriching the business ecosystem.

4. *Fostering a Culture of Excellence:* The impact of a Value Creator is not confined to their organization; it extends to the broader business community. Through their exemplary leadership and commitment to excellence, they set new standards for ethical conduct, innovation, and social responsibility. As other organizations strive to emulate their success, a culture of excellence is cultivated, raising the overall quality of products, services, and business practices.

5. *Spreading Social and Environmental Responsibility:* Value Creators recognize the significance of their role as corporate citizens. By integrating social and environmental responsibility into their business strategies, they become

advocates for positive change. Through philanthropic initiatives, sustainability practices, and community engagement, they inspire other businesses to prioritize social impact and contribute to the betterment of society.

6. *Building Trust and Reputation:* The Ripple Effect of a Value Creator's impact extends to stakeholders beyond their immediate customers and employees. Their unwavering commitment to value creation and ethical conduct earns them the trust and admiration of investors, partners, regulators, and the general public. This trust translates into a strong reputation that bolsters their influence and opens doors for future opportunities.

7. *Setting a Long-Term Vision:* Value Creators are driven by a long-term vision that transcends immediate gains. Their strategic foresight and perseverance in pursuing sustainable growth set an example for others to embrace a purpose-driven approach. By focusing on long-term goals, they instill a sense of stability and confidence in their organization, fostering an environment that values lasting impact over short-lived achievements.

8. *Empowering Future Generations:* The Ripple Effect of a Value Creator's impact extends to future generations. Their pioneering efforts and innovative solutions shape the business landscape for years to come. As the next generation of leaders and entrepreneurs looks back on their legacy, they find inspiration and guidance, carrying forward the torch of value-driven leadership.

In conclusion, the Ripple Effect of a Value Creator's impact is a testament to the profound influence one individual can have on the business world and society. Their visionary thinking, commitment to value, and transformative actions create a chain reaction that shapes industries, fosters innovation, and inspires positive change. The stories of extraordinary Value Creators serve as guiding beacons, motivating us to embrace visionary leadership, prioritize social responsibility, and drive revenue in ways that leave a lasting legacy of positive transformation. As we continue our journey through "THE VALUE

CREATOR: Driving Revenue and Impact in Business," let us be inspired by the far-reaching Ripple Effect of these remarkable individuals and embrace our potential to create value, impact lives, and make a difference in the world.

3

3

Becoming a Value Creator

This chapter delves into the transformative process of becoming a Value Creator – an exploration of how individuals can unlock their innate potential to drive revenue, create value, and make a positive impact on businesses, organizations, and society. In this chapter, we embark on a journey of self-discovery, skill development, and mindset transformation, guided by the principles that define exceptional Value Creators.

Becoming a Value Creator is not limited to a select few; it is a path open to every individual, regardless of their background or position. As we delve into this chapter, we recognize that the journey begins with recognizing the latent creativity, innovation, and purpose that reside within each of us.

We explore the essential qualities and characteristics that distinguish Value Creators and learn how to cultivate these attributes in our own lives. From visionary thinking and customer-centricity to resilience and adaptability, we uncover the building blocks that form the foundation of value-driven success.

Furthermore, the chapter serves as a guide to identifying opportunities where value creation thrives – from identifying unmet needs to embracing disruptive technologies and emerging trends. As we hone our skills and expertise, we gain the confidence to innovate and embrace calculated risks, knowing that failures are stepping stones on the path to growth.

Through real-life examples and illuminating insights, readers are inspired to embrace a growth mindset and a commitment to continuous learning. The journey of Becoming a Value Creator involves breaking free from conventional boundaries and embracing a culture of innovation and collaboration.

Moreover, we explore the profound impact of social and environmental responsibility in shaping the trajectory of a Value Creator's journey. By integrating purpose and sustainability into our endeavors, we contribute to a more equitable and sustainable future for businesses and society.

This chapter is a call to action – an invitation to every reader to awaken the Value Creator within themselves and become architects of positive change. It offers practical strategies, actionable insights, and inspiring stories to guide us on our path towards embracing visionary leadership, cultivating innovation, and driving revenue in ways that leave a lasting legacy.

As we immerse ourselves in the world of Becoming a Value Creator, may the wisdom and experiences of extraordinary individuals inspire us to unlock our potential, discover our purpose, and transform our lives and the lives of those around us. The journey to becoming a Value Creator awaits – let us embark on this transformative path and unleash the boundless possibilities of driving revenue and making a meaningful impact in the world of business and beyond.

Identifying Opportunities: Where Value Creation Thrives

At the heart of becoming a Value Creator lies the ability to identify opportunities where value creation thrives. Chapter 3 of "THE VALUE CREATOR: Driving Revenue and Impact in Business" explores the art of recognizing potential, uncovering unmet needs, and seizing opportunities that have the power to drive revenue and create a meaningful impact. In this chapter, we embark on a journey of exploration, innovation, and strategic thinking as we delve into the essential principles that guide us towards identifying and harnessing opportunities for value creation.

1. Understanding Market Trends and Customer Needs: Value Creators are keen observers of market trends and customer preferences. By staying attuned to shifts in consumer behavior, technological advancements, and industry developments, they identify gaps and emerging demands that present opportunities for innovation and value addition.

2. Embracing Disruptive Technologies: Value creation thrives in the realm of disruptive technologies. Value Creators are quick to embrace new technologies and leverage their transformative potential. They recognize that disruptive technologies can revolutionize industries and open doors to untapped markets.

3. Innovating Beyond Conventional Boundaries: Value Creators think beyond the status quo and challenge conventional norms. By embracing a mindset of continuous innovation, they develop solutions that solve complex problems and meet unmet needs, thus driving revenue and creating value where others might not have seen the potential.

4. Analyzing Data and Market Insights: Data-driven decision-making is a hallmark of a Value Creator's approach. They harness the power of data analytics and market insights to validate their assumptions, understand customer preferences, and identify opportunities for optimization and growth.

5. Identifying Pain Points and Unmet Needs: Value Creators are empathetic and attuned to the pain points of their customers and stakeholders. By identifying unmet needs and areas of improvement, they create products and services that resonate with their target audience, thus driving customer loyalty and market differentiation.

6. Collaborating and Networking: Value Creators recognize that collaboration and networking open doors to new opportunities. By building strategic partnerships and fostering collaborative relationships, they gain access to diverse expertise, resources, and markets that fuel their growth and impact.

7. Anticipating Future Trends: Value Creators possess a forward-thinking outlook that allows them to anticipate future trends and opportunities. By staying ahead of the curve, they position themselves to seize opportunities as they emerge, gaining a competitive advantage in dynamic markets.

8. Embracing Social and Environmental Challenges: Value Creators find value in addressing social and environmental challenges. By integrating social responsibility and sustainability into their business models, they not only make a positive impact on society but also attract socially conscious consumers and investors.

9. Navigating Disruptions and Uncertainties: Value Creators thrive in times of disruptions and uncertainties. They see challenges as opportunities for growth and are adept at adapting to changing circumstances, transforming setbacks into stepping stones for success.

10. Recognizing Talent and Expertise: Value Creators surround themselves with talented individuals and cultivate a culture of innovation and excellence. They recognize that their team's expertise is instrumental in identifying and seizing opportunities that lead to value creation.

In conclusion, identifying opportunities where value creation thrives is an essential aspect of becoming a Value Creator. This chapter serves as a guide to developing a keen sense of observation, a growth-oriented mindset, and an unwavering commitment to innovation and customer-centricity. By recognizing unmet needs, embracing disruption, and leveraging data-driven insights, we can unlock a world of opportunities to drive revenue, create impact, and leave a lasting legacy of value-driven success.

As we embrace the principles of identifying opportunities, we position ourselves to become catalysts for positive change and architects of transformation in the business world and society. Through strategic thinking, visionary leadership, and a deep understanding of customer needs, we embark on a transformative journey that paves the way for innovation, growth, and value creation in every endeavor we undertake. Let us seize the opportunities that lie ahead and embark on a path of becoming a Value Creator, igniting a ripple effect of positive impact in the world of business and beyond.

Cultivating a Value-Centric Mindset

In the pursuit of becoming a Value Creator, one of the most crucial elements is cultivating a value-centric mindset. This chapter explores the transformative power of mindset – the underlying beliefs, attitudes, and perspectives that shape our actions and drive us to create value in every endeavor. In this chapter, we embark on a journey of self-awareness, introspection, and intentional growth as we uncover the principles that define a value-centric mindset and its profound impact on driving revenue and creating meaningful impact.

1. Embracing Purpose and Meaning: At the core of a value-centric mindset lies a deep sense of purpose and meaning. Value Creators align their actions with a higher purpose, understanding that their endeavors serve not only their own interests but also the needs of their stakeholders and society at large. Embracing purpose infuses their work with passion and commitment, propelling them to make a meaningful impact.

2. Prioritizing Customer Value: A value-centric mindset revolves around prioritizing customer value. Value Creators understand that the success of their business is intrinsically linked to the satisfaction of their customers. By actively listening to customer feedback, anticipating their needs, and delivering exceptional experiences, they build lasting relationships that drive customer loyalty and revenue growth.

3. Embracing a Growth Mindset: Value Creators adopt a growth mindset, believing in their ability to learn, adapt, and improve continuously. They view challenges as opportunities for learning and growth, and setbacks as stepping stones to success. This mindset fosters resilience, innovation, and a willingness to take calculated risks in pursuit of value-driven outcomes.

4. Fostering Innovation and Creativity: A value-centric mindset nurtures creativity and encourages innovative thinking. Value Creators are unafraid to challenge the status quo, explore new ideas, and experiment with novel solutions. By fostering a culture of innovation, they empower their teams to think outside the box, leading to breakthroughs that drive revenue and create impact.

5. Demonstrating Ethical Leadership: Ethical leadership is a cornerstone of a value-centric mindset. Value Creators uphold integrity, transparency, and accountability in their actions, earning the trust and respect of their stakeholders. By adhering to ethical principles, they build a strong foundation of credibility and influence.

6. Practicing Empathy and Collaboration: Value Creators practice empathy, recognizing the diverse perspectives and needs of their stakeholders. By cultivating a collaborative and inclusive environment, they leverage the collective wisdom and creativity of their teams to drive value and foster a sense of ownership among their workforce.

7. *Valuing Continuous Learning:* Value Creators prioritize continuous learning and personal development. They stay informed about industry trends, emerging technologies, and best practices to stay at the forefront of value creation. This commitment to learning enables them to adapt to changing market dynamics and identify new opportunities for growth.

8. *Embracing Responsible Decision Making:* A value-centric mindset entails responsible decision-making. Value Creators consider the long-term impact of their choices on stakeholders, society, and the environment. They make informed decisions, weighing the consequences and benefits to drive sustainable growth and value creation.

9. *Celebrating Success and Learning from Failure:* A value-centric mindset acknowledges both success and failure as essential parts of the journey. Value Creators celebrate their achievements and milestones while viewing failures as opportunities to learn and improve. This perspective fosters a culture of continuous improvement and resilience.

10. *Embodying Gratitude and Appreciation:* A value-centric mindset is grounded in gratitude and appreciation. Value Creators recognize the contributions of their teams, customers, and stakeholders, expressing sincere gratitude for their support and commitment.

In conclusion, cultivating a value-centric mindset is a transformative journey that empowers individuals to become architects of positive change and catalysts for value creation. Through purpose-driven actions, customer-centricity, ethical leadership, and a commitment to continuous growth, we unlock our potential to drive revenue and create a meaningful impact in the world of business and beyond.

As we embrace the principles of a value-centric mindset, we become beacons of innovation, empathy, and responsible leadership. The impact of a value-centric mindset extends beyond financial success; it shapes the culture of organizations, inspires positive change in society, and leaves a legacy of value-driven success. Let us embark on this transformative journey, embodying a value-centric mindset as we drive revenue, create impact, and become the architects of a brighter, value-driven future.

Mastering Skills and Expertise for Maximum Impact

In the pursuit of becoming a Value Creator, mastery of skills and expertise is a vital aspect that propels individuals towards driving revenue and creating a maximum impact. This chapter delves into the transformative process of developing specialized knowledge, honing essential skills, and leveraging expertise to bring about profound change in businesses, organizations, and society as a whole. This chapter is a roadmap for individuals to unleash their potential by acquiring and refining the capabilities that elevate them to the realm of exceptional Value Creators.

1. Continuous Learning and Growth: A Value Creator is a lifelong learner, driven by a thirst for knowledge and personal development. They recognize that staying abreast of industry trends, emerging technologies, and best practices is paramount to their success. By dedicating themselves to continuous learning, they acquire new insights and perspectives that enable them to stay ahead of the competition.

2. Technical and Industry Expertise: Mastery of technical skills and industry-specific knowledge is a hallmark of a Value Creator. By immersing themselves in their field of expertise, they gain a deep understanding of the nuances and intricacies that drive value creation. This expertise positions them as trusted advisors and thought leaders, attracting customers, partners, and investors.

3. Leadership and Emotional Intelligence: Effective leadership is an essential skill for a Value Creator. They inspire and motivate their teams, fostering a culture of innovation, collaboration, and accountability. Furthermore, they possess emotional intelligence, understanding the needs and emotions of others, and navigating interpersonal dynamics with empathy and grace.

4. Problem-Solving and Critical Thinking: Value Creators are adept problem-solvers who approach challenges with analytical rigor and creativity. They can identify root causes, devise effective solutions, and make data-driven decisions that lead to tangible results.

5. Communication and Persuasion: A Value Creator's impact hinges on their ability to communicate ideas, visions, and strategies effectively. They are compelling storytellers who can articulate their value proposition and persuade stakeholders to rally behind their cause.

6. Innovation and Creativity: Value Creators are trailblazers who embrace innovation and creativity. They challenge conventional thinking, explore new ideas, and experiment with novel approaches. Their innovative mindset leads to the development of unique products, services, and business models that set them apart from the competition.

7. Financial Acumen: Mastery of financial acumen is critical for a Value Creator to make informed business decisions. They understand financial statements, cash flow management, and investment strategies, ensuring sustainable growth and profitability.

8. Negotiation and Conflict Resolution: Value Creators are skilled negotiators who can forge mutually beneficial partnerships and agreements. Moreover, they are adept at conflict resolution, fostering constructive dialogue and resolving disputes to maintain harmonious relationships.

9. Tech Savviness: In the digital age, tech savviness is a crucial skill for a Value Creator. They embrace technological advancements, harnessing the power of data analytics, artificial intelligence, and digital marketing to optimize business operations and drive revenue growth.

10. Adaptability and Resilience: Value Creators possess the resilience to persevere in the face of challenges and uncertainties. They adapt to changing market dynamics, evolving customer preferences, and industry disruptions, transforming setbacks into opportunities for growth.

In conclusion, mastering skills and expertise is a transformative journey that enables individuals to unleash their potential as Value Creators. By committing to continuous learning, acquiring technical and industry knowledge, honing leadership and emotional intelligence, and fostering a culture of innovation, individuals position themselves to drive revenue and create maximum impact in their chosen domain.

As we embrace the principles of mastery, we become architects of positive change, catalysts for innovation, and drivers of growth. The impact of mastering skills and expertise extends beyond individual success; it contributes to the collective advancement of businesses, organizations, and society as a whole. Let us embark on this transformative journey, mastering our skills and expertise to become exceptional Value Creators and shape a future defined by value-driven success.

4

4

Driving Revenue as a Value Creator

This chapter is a comprehensive guide that unravels the strategic approaches, innovative thinking, and customer-centric practices that propel individuals towards achieving revenue growth and sustainable success.

In this chapter, readers will explore the multifaceted strategies employed by Value Creators to think outside the box, seize opportunities, and navigate challenges to maximize revenue. From leveraging disruptive technologies to embracing data-driven decision-making, the chapter showcases how Value Creators stay at the forefront of their industries and drive tangible financial results.

Moreover, the chapter emphasizes the significance of customer value and experience in revenue generation. Readers will gain insights into how Value Creators prioritize customer needs, deliver exceptional experiences, and build lasting relationships that foster customer loyalty and drive revenue growth.

Additionally, the chapter examines the pivotal role of innovation and creativity in revenue generation. Through real-life examples and illuminating case studies, readers will witness how Value Creators cultivate a culture of innovation, explore new markets, and develop groundbreaking products and services that capture new revenue streams.

Furthermore, the chapter uncovers the power of collaboration and strategic partnerships in driving revenue. Value Creators recognize the value of collaboration with other businesses and organizations to expand their reach, access new markets, and unlock synergistic opportunities that drive mutual growth.

In conclusion, "THE VALUE CREATOR: Driving Revenue and Impact in Business" is a transformative exploration of the strategies, principles, and practices that empower individuals to become catalysts for revenue growth. As readers immerse themselves in this chapter, they will gain valuable insights and actionable strategies to drive revenue as a Value Creator, leaving a lasting impact on their businesses, organizations, and industries. The journey of revenue generation awaits, and with the wisdom and inspiration from this chapter, readers will be equipped to unleash their potential and embrace the transformative power of value-driven success.

Strategies for Revenue Generation: Thinking Outside the Box

In the pursuit of becoming a Value Creator, one of the most powerful tools at our disposal is the ability to think outside the box when it comes to revenue generation. This chapter explores the art of innovative thinking and strategic approaches that propel individuals towards maximizing revenue and achieving sustainable growth. In this chapter, we embark on a journey of exploration, creativity, and unconventional strategies as we uncover the transformative power of thinking outside the box.

1. Embrace Disruptive Technologies: Value Creators understand that embracing disruptive technologies can unlock new revenue streams. They harness the potential of artificial intelligence, blockchain, the Internet of Things (IoT), and other cutting-edge technologies to create innovative products, services, and business models that meet evolving customer needs.

2. Pivot and Diversify: Thinking outside the box requires the ability to pivot and diversify when necessary. Value Creators keenly observe market trends and customer preferences, and they are quick to adapt their offerings to align with changing demands. By diversifying their product or service portfolio, they mitigate risks and tap into multiple revenue sources.

3. Subscription and Membership Models: Subscription-based and membership models are powerful strategies for consistent revenue generation. Value Creators leverage these models to create recurring revenue streams while offering added value to customers in the form of exclusive benefits, personalized experiences, and ongoing support.

4. Freemium and Upselling: The freemium model, where basic services are offered for free with the option to upgrade to premium features, is another innovative strategy employed by Value Creators. Upselling complementary products or a service to existing customers is also a tactic that maximizes revenue and customer satisfaction.

5. Target New Markets and Segments: Value Creators identify and target new markets and customer segments to expand their reach and tap into unexplored opportunities. By understanding the unique needs of these markets, they tailor their offerings and marketing strategies to resonate with different audiences.

6. Strategic Partnerships and Alliances: Collaborating with other businesses and organizations through strategic partnerships and alliances is a hallmark of a Value Creator's revenue generation strategy. Such collaborations offer access to new markets, shared resources, and complementary expertise, driving mutual growth and revenue.

7. Monetizing Data and Intellectual Property: Value Creators leverage the value of data and intellectual property to generate revenue. They monetize data insights by offering analytics and market intelligence services, and they protect and commercialize their innovations through licensing and patents.

8. Exceptional Customer Experience: Providing an exceptional customer experience is not only a key differentiator but also a revenue generation strategy. Value Creators prioritize customer satisfaction, delighting customers with personalized experiences, prompt support, and seamless interactions that drive customer loyalty and word-of-mouth referrals.

9. Invest in Marketing and Branding: Value Creators recognize the importance of investing in marketing and branding to build a strong presence in the market. They communicate their value proposition effectively, create compelling brand stories, and engage in targeted marketing efforts to attract and retain customers.

10. Launch Limited-Time Offers and Exclusives: Limited-time offers and exclusives create a sense of urgency and exclusivity, encouraging customers to take action and make purchases. Value Creators strategically leverage these promotions to drive short-term revenue spikes and boost customer engagement.

In conclusion, This chapter showcases the strategies that enable individuals to think outside the box and unleash their potential as revenue generators. By embracing disruptive technologies, diversifying offerings, targeting new markets, and fostering strategic partnerships, Value Creators propel their businesses and organizations to new heights of revenue growth and impact.

Thinking outside the box empowers us to innovate, seize untapped opportunities, and challenge conventional norms, positioning us as architects of change and drivers of value creation. As we immerse ourselves in the world of innovative strategies, we embark on a transformative journey to maximize revenue, create lasting impact, and leave a legacy of value-driven success in the dynamic and ever-evolving business landscape.

Leveraging Innovation and Creativity for Sustainable Growth

Innovation and creativity are the cornerstones of sustainable growth for businesses and organizations. This chapter explores the transformative power of innovation and creativity as essential strategies employed by Value Creators to achieve sustainable growth. In this chapter, we embark on a journey of exploration, ideation, and implementation, uncovering how innovation and creativity fuel revenue generation, customer engagement, and long-term success.

1. *Cultivating a Culture of Innovation:* Value Creators recognize that innovation starts from within. They foster a culture that encourages and rewards creativity, risk-taking, and experimentation. By creating an environment where team members feel empowered to share ideas and challenge the status quo, Value Creators unlock a wellspring of innovative thinking.

2. *Embracing Emerging Technologies:* Innovation and sustainable growth are closely linked to the adoption of emerging technologies. Value Creators stay at the forefront of technological advancements, leveraging tools such as artificial intelligence, automation, and data analytics to optimize processes, personalize customer experiences, and identify new revenue opportunities.

3. *Design Thinking and Customer-Centricity:* Value Creators employ design thinking principles to understand customer needs deeply. By empathizing with their customers and involving them in the product development process, they create solutions that truly resonate with their target audience, driving

customer satisfaction and loyalty.

4. Encouraging Intrapreneurship: Intrapreneurship is a powerful driver of innovation within organizations. Value Creators encourage intrapreneurship by empowering employees to act as entrepreneurs within the company, supporting them in exploring new ideas and initiatives that align with the organization's vision and goals.

5. Rapid Prototyping and Iterative Development: Value Creators embrace rapid prototyping and iterative development to bring products and services to market quickly. They gather feedback early in the development process and use it to make continuous improvements, ensuring that their offerings meet evolving customer needs and preferences.

6. Open Innovation and Collaboration: Value Creators recognize the value of open innovation and collaboration. They collaborate with external partners, startups, and industry experts to gain fresh perspectives, access new technologies, and explore joint ventures that drive mutual growth.

7. Sustainable Business Practices: Sustainability and innovation go hand in hand for Value Creators. They integrate sustainable practices into their business models, supply chains, and operations, appealing to socially conscious customers and investors while making a positive impact on the environment.

8. Diversification of Revenue Streams: Innovation enables Value Creators to diversify revenue streams, reducing reliance on a single product or market. By expanding their product/service offerings or tapping into new markets, they create resilient business models that thrive in dynamic market conditions.

9. Customer-Driven Problem Solving: Value Creators use creativity to address customer pain points proactively. They leverage insights from customer feedback, data analysis, and market research to develop solutions that directly address the challenges their customers face, driving customer satisfaction and loyalty.

10. Agile and Adaptive Strategies: Innovation empowers Value Creators to remain agile and adaptive. They pivot quickly in response to changing market dynamics and customer preferences, ensuring their strategies remain relevant and effective in a rapidly evolving business landscape.

In conclusion, This chapter celebrates the transformative power of innovation and creativity as catalysts for sustainable growth. By cultivating a culture of innovation, embracing emerging technologies, and prioritizing customer-centricity, Value Creators forge paths to success that are fueled by fresh ideas and continuous improvement.

Leveraging innovation and creativity not only drives revenue generation but also fosters customer loyalty, attracts top talent, and positions businesses and organizations as pioneers in their industries. As we embrace the principles of innovation and creativity, we unlock our potential as Value Creators, shaping a future defined by sustainable growth, positive impact, and lasting success in the world of business and beyond.

Navigating Challenges and Turning Them into Opportunities

In the journey of becoming a Value Creator, challenges are inevitable. This chapter explores the art of navigating challenges and transforming them into opportunities for growth and success. In this chapter, we embark on a transformative exploration of resilience, adaptability, and strategic thinking as we uncover how Value Creators harness the power of challenges to drive innovation, build resilience, and create positive impact.

1. Embrace a Growth Mindset: Value Creators approach challenges with a growth mindset – they view setbacks as opportunities to learn and improve. By embracing a mindset that perceives challenges as stepping stones for growth, they are more open to exploring alternative solutions and turning adversity into a catalyst for positive change.

2. Identify Root Causes: When faced with challenges, Value Creators seek to identify the root causes rather than merely addressing the symptoms. By understanding the underlying issues, they can develop more effective strategies and solutions that prevent similar challenges from arising in the future.

3. Iterate and Adapt: Challenges often require flexible and adaptive approaches. Value Creators iterate and adapt their strategies based on real-time feedback and changing circumstances. This iterative approach enables them to respond swiftly and effectively to challenges, refining their solutions along the way.

4. Collaborate and Seek Support: Value Creators understand the value of collaboration and seek support from their teams, partners, and stakeholders when navigating challenges. By involving others in problem-solving, they harness collective wisdom, diverse perspectives, and shared expertise, leading to more robust and innovative solutions.

5. Turn Constraints into Innovation: Challenges can present constraints, but Value Creators transform these limitations into opportunities for innovation. They see constraints as catalysts for creativity, inspiring them to develop inventive solutions and disruptive approaches that set them apart from the competition.

6. Stay Customer-Centric: In the face of challenges, Value Creators remain focused on their customers' needs and preferences. By staying customer-centric, they can tailor their responses to address customer pain points effectively, ensuring that their solutions resonate with their target audience.

7. Seek Opportunities for Growth: Value Creators approach challenges as opportunities for growth and improvement. They embrace the chance to enhance their skills, systems, and processes, positioning themselves for long-term success in the face of ever-changing market dynamics.

8. Build Resilience: Challenges can test an individual's or organization's resilience, but Value Creators are adept at bouncing back from setbacks. They build resilience by fostering a positive organizational culture, providing support to their teams, and maintaining a long-term vision that sustains them during challenging times.

9. Learn from Failures: Value Creators view failures as valuable learning experiences. They analyze their mistakes, extract insights, and use this knowledge to inform future decision-making. Learning from failures empowers them to avoid repeating the same missteps and to continually improve their strategies.

10. Turn Challenges into Opportunities: Above all, Value Creators have a unique ability to turn challenges into opportunities. They recognize that challenges often present unmet needs and gaps in the market. By addressing these challenges creatively, they create new products, services, or business models that meet customer demands and drive revenue growth.

In conclusion, This chapter celebrates the transformative power of navigating challenges and turning them into opportunities for growth and innovation. As we embrace the principles of resilience, adaptability, and customer-centricity, we unlock our potential to become Value Creators who thrive amidst adversity and create lasting impact.

Navigating challenges is not about avoiding obstacles, but rather about leveraging them as stepping stones towards success. With a growth mindset, collaborative spirit, and strategic thinking, we transform challenges into fertile ground for innovation, driving revenue, and creating positive change in the dynamic and ever-evolving world of business and beyond. Let us embrace challenges as catalysts for growth and embark on a transformative journey as Value Creators who shape a future defined by resilience, innovation, and value-driven success.

5

5

Measuring and Quantifying Impact

In this chapter, we explore the transformative power of data-driven decision-making and performance metrics as essential tools employed by Value Creators to gauge the effectiveness of their strategies and initiatives. Measuring and quantifying impact is an integral part of the value creation process, allowing individuals and organizations to assess their progress, optimize their efforts, and drive sustainable growth.

In the pursuit of becoming a Value Creator, understanding the tangible outcomes and the ripple effect of one's actions is essential. This chapter serves as a comprehensive guide that unravels the methods and frameworks used by Value Creators to track key performance indicators, analyze data, and derive meaningful insights from their impact.

From revenue growth and customer retention to social and environmental impact, this chapter showcases how Value Creators leverage data analytics and metrics to make informed decisions that align with their mission, vision, and long-term goals. By measuring and quantifying impact, Value Creators gain a holistic view of their contributions, enabling them to refine their strategies and ensure that every action generates value for their stakeholders and society as a whole.

As we dive into the realm of data-driven evaluation and impact assessment, this chapter empowers individuals and organizations to become more accountable, transparent, and purpose-driven in their pursuit of value creation. The transformative potential of measuring impact lies not only in optimizing revenue generation but also in fostering a positive and sustainable impact on the world.

We will explore the frameworks and tools used by Value Creators to assess financial performance, customer satisfaction, social responsibility, and environmental sustainability. By understanding how to measure and quantify impact effectively, readers will gain valuable insights to enhance their decision-making, optimize their strategies, and leave a lasting legacy of value-driven success in the global business landscape.

Metrics and Analytics: Tracking Value Creation and Revenue Growth

In the pursuit of becoming a Value Creator, metrics and analytics play a pivotal role in tracking and quantifying the impact of one's actions on revenue growth and value creation. This chapter looks into the transformative power of data-driven decision-making and performance tracking as essential tools employed by Value Creators to measure their success and optimize their strategies.

1. Key Performance Indicators (KPIs): Value Creators identify and track Key Performance Indicators (KPIs) that align with their goals and reflect their value creation efforts. These KPIs may include revenue growth, customer acquisition and retention rates, profit margins, customer satisfaction scores, social impact metrics, and more. By monitoring KPIs, Value Creators gain real-time insights into their progress and can make data-driven decisions to steer their initiatives in the right direction.

2. Customer Lifetime Value (CLV): Understanding the Customer Lifetime Value is crucial for Value Creators to assess the long-term revenue potential of their customer base. By quantifying the value of a customer over their entire relationship with the business, Value Creators can prioritize customer retention strategies and enhance customer experiences to maximize revenue and customer loyalty.

3. Return on Investment (ROI): ROI is a fundamental metric used by Value Creators to evaluate the financial impact of their investments and initiatives. By comparing the gains from an investment to its costs, Value Creators can determine whether a particular strategy or project is delivering the expected returns and adjust their resource allocation accordingly.

4. Customer Feedback and Surveys: Value Creators actively seek customer feedback through surveys and direct interactions to gauge customer satisfaction and identify areas for improvement. Customer feedback provides valuable insights into the effectiveness of products, services, and overall customer experiences, guiding Value Creators in enhancing value for their customers.

5. Social Impact Metrics: Beyond financial metrics, Value Creators track social impact metrics to assess the influence of their actions on communities and society. These metrics may include the number of jobs created, environmental sustainability efforts, charitable contributions, and other indicators that showcase their commitment to social responsibility.

6. Data Visualization and Dashboards: Value Creators leverage data visualization and dashboards to transform complex data sets into clear, visual representations. These tools enable Value Creators to interpret data easily, identify patterns, and communicate their findings to stakeholders effectively.

7. A/B Testing and Experimentation: Value Creators employ A/B testing and experimentation to test different strategies, marketing campaigns, and product features. By comparing the performance of variations, they can identify the most effective approaches that drive revenue growth and value creation.

8. Market and Competitive Analysis: Value Creators conduct thorough market and competitive analysis to benchmark their performance against industry peers and identify areas where they can gain a competitive edge. This analysis helps them stay ahead of market trends and align their strategies with customer demands.

9. Customer Segmentation: Customer segmentation allows Value Creators to divide their customer base into distinct groups based on demographics, behaviors, and preferences. By understanding the unique needs of each segment, Value Creators can tailor their offerings and marketing strategies to optimize revenue generation.

10. Forecasting and Predictive Analytics: Value Creators leverage forecasting and predictive analytics to anticipate future trends and potential challenges. By using historical data and advanced algorithms, they can make informed decisions that drive revenue growth and capitalize on emerging opportunities.

In conclusion, By adopting data-driven decision-making, Value Creators gain a comprehensive understanding of their impact, optimize their strategies, and make informed choices that align with their mission and vision.

Metrics and analytics are not just tools for evaluating past performance; they are essential navigational tools that guide Value Creators towards a future defined by sustainable growth and value-driven success. As we embrace the principles of data-driven evaluation and performance tracking, we empower ourselves to become exceptional Value Creators, leaving a lasting impact on businesses, organizations, and society as a whole.

Data-Driven Decision Making: Optimizing Performance

In the realm of value creation, data-driven decision-making is a game-changing approach that empowers individuals and organizations to optimize performance and drive sustainable growth. This part dig into the transformative power of data-driven decision-making as a critical tool employed by Value Creators to extract meaningful insights from data, identify opportunities, and aligns strategies with the ever-changing business landscape.

1. Harnessing the Power of Data: Value Creators recognize that data is an invaluable asset that holds the key to unlocking hidden opportunities and understanding customer behavior. They leverage various data sources, including customer feedback, sales figures, market trends, and social media analytics, to gain comprehensive insights into their operations and customer base.

2. Identifying Patterns and Trends: Data-driven decision-making enables Value Creators to identify patterns and trends that may go unnoticed without data analysis. By spotting correlations and trends, they can make informed predictions and adjust their strategies to align with market demands and customer preferences.

3. Real-Time Decision Making: In today's fast-paced business environment, real-time decision-making is essential for staying competitive. Value Creators leverage data analytics tools to access up-to-the-minute information, empowering them to make agile decisions that capitalize on emerging opportunities and mitigate potential risks.

4. Customer-Centric Insights: Data-driven decision-making places the customer at the core of business strategies. Value Creators analyze customer data to understand their needs, pain points, and preferences, enabling them to tailor products, services, and marketing efforts that resonate with their target audience.

5. *Business Process Optimization*: Data-driven insights extend beyond customer-centric strategies. Value Creators use data to optimize internal processes, identify inefficiencies, and enhance productivity. This continuous improvement approach ensures that resources are allocated effectively, leading to cost savings and enhanced performance.

6. *Risk Mitigation*: Data-driven decision-making helps Value Creators anticipate and mitigate risks effectively. By analyzing historical data and market trends, they can identify potential challenges and develop contingency plans to navigate uncertainties and safeguard their businesses.

7. *Personalization and Customer Experience*: Personalization is a key element of data-driven decision-making. Value Creators use customer data to create personalized experiences that foster customer loyalty and drive repeat business. From personalized recommendations to tailored marketing campaigns, personalization enhances the overall customer experience.

8. *Predictive Analytics:* Value Creators leverage predictive analytics to forecast future trends and customer behavior. This enables them to proactively address customer needs, plan inventory and resources, and capitalize on emerging market opportunities.

9. *Measuring Impact and ROI:* Data-driven decision-making enables Value Creators to measure the impact of their initiatives and investments accurately. By quantifying the Return on Investment (ROI) of various strategies, they can allocate resources to high-impact initiatives and optimize revenue generation.

10. *Continuous Improvement:* Data-driven decision-making fosters a culture of continuous improvement within organizations. Value Creators use data

analytics to monitor the outcomes of their strategies and iterate on their approaches to achieve better results continuously.

In conclusion, This observed the transformative power of data-driven decision-making as a cornerstone of value creation. By embracing data as a strategic asset, Value Creators gain a competitive advantage, optimize performance, and drive sustainable growth.

Data-driven decision-making is not just about interpreting data; it is about cultivating a data-driven mindset that guides every aspect of decision-making, from strategy formulation to customer engagement. As we embrace the principles of data-driven decision-making, we equip ourselves to become exceptional Value Creators who leverage data as a powerful tool to navigate complexities, uncover opportunities, and create a lasting impact on businesses, organizations, and society as a whole.

Inspiring Others to Follow the Value Creator's Lead

In the journey of becoming a Value Creator, one of the most profound impacts lies in the ability to inspire and empower others to follow one's lead. Chapter 5 of "THE VALUE CREATOR: Driving Revenue and Impact in Business" explores the transformative power of leadership, influence, and vision as essential traits employed by Value Creators to inspire individuals, teams, and organizations to embrace the values of value creation and drive positive change.

1. Authentic Leadership: Value Creators lead by example, demonstrating authenticity, integrity, and a genuine passion for value creation. They embody the principles they advocate, establishing themselves as credible and trustworthy leaders that others aspire to emulate.

2. Communicating a Compelling Vision: A compelling vision is a cornerstone of inspiring leadership. Value Creators articulate a clear and inspiring vision that captures the hearts and minds of their teams and stakeholders. This shared purpose fosters a sense of purpose and unity, aligning efforts towards a common goal.

3. Empowering Others: Value Creators empower others to realize their full potential. They encourage creativity, innovation, and independent thinking, creating an environment where team members feel valued and confident to take initiative.

4. Recognizing and Celebrating Success: Value Creators understand the importance of recognizing and celebrating the achievements of their teams. By acknowledging their contributions and celebrating milestones, they foster a culture of appreciation and motivation that drives continuous improvement.

5. Mentoring and Coaching: Value Creators are not only visionary leaders but also mentors and coaches to their teams. They invest time in developing the skills and capabilities of their team members, fostering a culture of learning and growth.

6. Building a Supportive Culture: Value Creators foster a supportive and collaborative culture within their organizations. They encourage open communication, teamwork, and knowledge-sharing, creating an environment where ideas are freely exchanged and innovation thrives.

7. Demonstrating Resilience: In the face of challenges, Value Creators exhibit resilience and perseverance. Their ability to navigate obstacles and bounce back from setbacks inspires others to remain steadfast in their pursuit of value-driven success.

8. Leading by Purpose: Value Creators lead with purpose, communicating not only the "what" and "how" but also the "why" behind their initiatives. This sense of purpose ignites passion and dedication in their teams, reinforcing the commitment to creating meaningful impact.

9. Being Adaptable: Value Creators embrace adaptability and agility. They lead by example in embracing change and are quick to adjust strategies in response to market dynamics and customer needs.

10. Sharing Success Stories: Value Creators share success stories and real-life examples of the positive impact of value creation. By showcasing tangible outcomes and inspiring stories of transformation, they reinforce the importance of value creation and its potential to drive meaningful change.

In conclusion, This chapter acknowledges the transformative power of inspiring others to follow the Value Creator's lead. As we embrace the principles of authentic leadership, empowering others, and communicating a compelling vision, we unlock our potential to become catalysts for positive change and value-driven success.

Inspiring others to follow the Value Creator's lead is not about dictating or imposing; it is about fostering an environment where individuals are encouraged to unleash their potential, take ownership of their ideas, and embrace the principles of value creation. As we inspire and empower others, we create a ripple effect of positive impact that extends beyond our organizations, enriching the lives of individuals, businesses, and society as a whole. Let us lead with purpose, inspire with authenticity, and ignite a collective passion for value creation, shaping a future defined by sustainable growth and lasting change.

6

6

The History of Value Creators - Inspiring Legacies for Modern Entrepreneurs

In the annals of history, there are remarkable instances of visionary individuals who, through their groundbreaking contributions to the business world, have left an indelible mark on society and inspired generations of entrepreneurs. From ancient innovators to modern tech titans, their stories serve as beacons of inspiration, illuminating the transformative power of value-driven principles and igniting a spark within aspiring entrepreneurs to take positive actionable steps in their own ventures.

One such iconic figure is Andrew Carnegie, the 19th-century steel magnate, and philanthropist. Carnegie's journey from a poor immigrant to a business titan showcases the potential for resilience and determination to pave the way for unprecedented success. His visionary leadership and adoption of the Bessemer process revolutionized the steel industry, transforming it into a cornerstone of industrialization. Inspired by Carnegie's legacy, modern entrepreneurs can embrace perseverance and a long-term vision to navigate challenges and build enduring businesses.

Another historical luminary is Coco Chanel, the trailblazing fashion designer who revolutionized the world of haute couture. Chanel's daring and innovation disrupted the norms of her time, introducing comfortable and elegant women's fashion that embraced practicality and style. Her story serves as a reminder to modern entrepreneurs to challenge conventions, embrace creativity, and create innovative solutions that resonate with their target audience.

In the modern era, the visionary leadership of Steve Jobs at Apple Inc. continues to inspire entrepreneurs worldwide. Jobs' relentless pursuit of excellence and focus on customer experience laid the foundation for Apple's extraordinary success. His commitment to seamless integration of technology and design has left an indelible mark on the tech industry, inspiring entrepreneurs to prioritize user-centric innovation and deliver exceptional experiences to their customers.

Elon Musk, the entrepreneur behind Tesla, SpaceX, and other ventures, embodies the spirit of innovation and risk-taking. Musk's audacious vision of a sustainable future and his relentless drive to disrupt industries have sparked global interest and admiration. His story encourages modern entrepreneurs to embrace boldness, embrace audacious goals, and work tirelessly to bring their vision to life, regardless of the obstacles they face.

These historical antecedents underscore the timeless principles of value-driven leadership, innovation, and customer-centricity that resonate with entrepreneurs across ages. Each visionary figure showcases the transformative potential of perseverance, creativity, and a passion for creating meaningful impact.

As aspiring entrepreneurs read the stories of these legendary value creators, they are inspired to take positive actionable steps in their own ventures. They learn the importance of fostering a growth mindset, staying resilient in the face of challenges, and embracing innovation to drive their businesses forward. The legacies of these visionary individuals not only ignite a desire to emulate their success but also instill a commitment to building businesses that contribute positively to the world.

In conclusion, the history of value creators is replete with inspiring stories of visionary leaders who have transformed industries, impacted societies, and left enduring legacies. From Andrew Carnegie's resilience to Coco Chanel's boldness, and from Steve Jobs' customer-centric innovation to Elon Musk's audacity, each figure offers invaluable lessons for modern entrepreneurs. By embracing the principles and values exemplified by these legendary value creators, aspiring entrepreneurs can take positive actionable steps towards creating businesses that drive revenue, make a lasting impact, and shape a brighter future for generations to come.

Lessons from Legendary Value Creators Throughout History

Throughout history, legendary value creators have left an indelible mark on the business world, inspiring generations with their innovative thinking, visionary leadership, and unwavering commitment to creating value. These iconic figures offer valuable lessons for modern entrepreneurs, encouraging them to embrace resilience, creativity, and customer-centricity in their pursuit of success. Let us explore some of the invaluable lessons from legendary value creators and the real-life examples that demonstrate their enduring impact on the business landscape.

1. Resilience in the Face of Adversity:

Example: Thomas Edison - Often referred to as the "Wizard of Menlo Park," Thomas Edison faced numerous failures and setbacks while inventing the electric light bulb. Despite thousands of unsuccessful attempts, he remained persistent and famously stated, "I have not failed. I've just found 10,000 ways that won't work." Edison's unwavering resilience eventually led to the successful invention of the practical electric light bulb, revolutionizing the world of lighting and electrical technology.

Lesson: Aspiring entrepreneurs can learn from Edison's determination to persevere in the face of adversity. Embracing failures as opportunities for growth and learning is essential in the journey of value creation and business success.

2. Innovation and Disruption:

Example: Steve Jobs - Co-founder of Apple Inc., Steve Jobs was a visionary leader known for his relentless pursuit of innovation and disruptive thinking. He revolutionized the technology industry with groundbreaking products like the iPhone, iPad, and MacBook, redefining the way people interact with technology.

Lesson: Jobs' commitment to pushing the boundaries of technology showcases the importance of staying at the forefront of innovation. Modern entrepreneurs can learn from Jobs' customer-centric approach and focus on delivering products and experiences that exceed expectations.

3. Customer-Centricity and Empathy:

Example: Henry Ford - Henry Ford, founder of Ford Motor Company, is renowned for his customer-centric approach to manufacturing automobiles. By introducing assembly line production techniques, Ford was able to produce affordable cars, making automobiles accessible to the masses.

Lesson: Ford's emphasis on meeting customer needs and making products accessible to a broader audience demonstrates the significance of empathizing with customers. Understanding their pain points and desires is vital in developing products and services that resonate with the target market.

4. Social Responsibility and Philanthropy:

Example: Andrew Carnegie - The 19th-century steel magnate, Andrew

Carnegie, exemplified the importance of social responsibility and philanthropy. After amassing great wealth, he dedicated his later years to philanthropic efforts, establishing libraries, universities, and cultural institutions to benefit society.

Lesson: Carnegie's commitment to giving back to society showcases the impact of socially responsible business practices. Modern entrepreneurs can draw inspiration from his philanthropic legacy and consider how their businesses can contribute positively to their communities.

5. Vision and Boldness:

Example: Elon Musk - A modern-day visionary, Elon Musk, CEO of Tesla and SpaceX, is known for his audacious goals of revolutionizing transportation and space exploration. His pursuit of sustainable energy solutions and interplanetary travel has captured the imagination of the world.

Lesson: Musk's bold vision demonstrates the importance of thinking big and pursuing ambitious goals. Entrepreneurs can learn from his determination to challenge established norms and take calculated risks to drive their ventures forward.

6. Creativity and Differentiation:

Example: Coco Chanel - The legendary fashion designer, Coco Chanel, disrupted the fashion industry with her innovative designs that emphasized comfort, simplicity, and elegance. She introduced iconic products like the little black dress and Chanel No. 5 perfume, which continue to define elegance and style.

Lesson: Chanel's creative approach to fashion underscores the significance of differentiation in business. Entrepreneurs can draw inspiration from her unique style and focus on developing products or services that stand out in the market.

In conclusion, the lessons from legendary value creators are as relevant today as they were in the past. Resilience, innovation, customer-centricity, social responsibility, vision, and creativity are timeless principles that drive business success. Real-life examples of figures like Thomas Edison, Steve Jobs, Henry Ford, Andrew Carnegie, Elon Musk, and Coco Chanel exemplify these principles and inspire modern entrepreneurs to take positive actionable steps in their own ventures. By embracing the spirit of these legendary value creators, aspiring entrepreneurs can create meaningful impact, drive revenue, and leave their own enduring legacy in the business world.

How Their Legacy Continues to Shape Modern Business

The legacy of legendary value creators continues to exert a profound influence on modern business practices and serves as a guiding beacon for entrepreneurs and organizations worldwide. Their innovative thinking, visionary leadership, and commitment to creating value have shaped the business landscape, inspiring contemporary leaders to follow in their footsteps. Let us explore how the legacy of these iconic figures continues to shape modern business, along with real-life examples that demonstrate their enduring impact.

1. Embracing Innovation and Disruption:
   Example: Apple Inc. - The legacy of Steve Jobs, the co-founder of Apple Inc., continues to drive the company's approach to innovation and disruption. Apple has consistently introduced groundbreaking products, from the iPod to the iPhone and beyond, redefining industries and setting new standards for user experience and design. Jobs' visionary principles laid the foundation for Apple's culture of innovation, inspiring other companies to push the boundaries of what is possible in technology and beyond.

2. Customer-Centricity and Experience:
   Example: Amazon - Jeff Bezos, the founder of Amazon, embodies the

customer-centric principles of legendary value creators. Amazon's success can be attributed to its relentless focus on providing exceptional customer experiences. Bezos famously stated, "We see our customers as invited guests to a party, and we are the hosts. It's our job every day to make every important aspect of the customer experience a little bit better." This customer-centric approach has set Amazon apart and influenced countless other businesses to prioritize customer satisfaction.

3. Sustainable and Socially Responsible Business Practices:

Example: Patagonia - Yvon Chouinard, the founder of outdoor apparel brand Patagonia, is an advocate for sustainable and socially responsible business practices. Patagonia's commitment to environmental conservation and ethical sourcing resonates with consumers who value sustainability. Chouinard's legacy has spurred a movement toward sustainable and ethical practices in the fashion industry and beyond, inspiring other businesses to take responsibility for their impact on the planet and society.

4. Disrupting Traditional Industries:

Example: Uber - Travis Kalanick and Garrett Camp disrupted the traditional taxi industry with the founding of Uber. By leveraging technology to create a platform that connects drivers with riders, Uber transformed the transportation sector. This disruptive approach to business has influenced the rise of the sharing economy, with various companies adopting similar models in different industries.

5. Fostering a Culture of Innovation:

Example: Google - The culture of innovation at Google is deeply influenced by the company's co-founders, Larry Page, and Sergey Brin. Their vision for organizing the world's information and making it universally accessible continues to drive Google's commitment to groundbreaking technologies and products. The company's "20% time" policy, which allows employees to dedicate a portion of their workweek to personal projects, fosters a culture of creativity and exploration that has yielded significant innovations.

6. Pursuit of Audacious Goals:

Example: SpaceX - Elon Musk, the founder of SpaceX, is renowned for his audacious vision of making space travel more accessible and eventually colonizing Mars. SpaceX's achievements, such as the development of reusable rockets, have revolutionized space exploration. Musk's determination to push the boundaries of what is possible has inspired the aerospace industry and captivated the world's imagination.

7. Impactful Corporate Social Responsibility:

Example: TOMS - Blake Mycoskie, the founder of TOMS, created a business model that aligns profitability with social impact. For every pair of shoes sold, TOMS donates a pair to a child in need. This model has not only transformed the footwear industry but has also inspired other companies to incorporate social responsibility into their core business practices.

In conclusion, the legacy of legendary value creators continues to shape modern business in profound ways. Their visionary principles, commitment to innovation, customer-centricity, sustainability, and disruption have left an enduring impact on the business landscape. Real-life examples of companies like Apple, Amazon, Patagonia, Uber, Google, SpaceX, and TOMS demonstrate how the principles of these iconic figures are reflected in contemporary business practices.

By embracing the values and approaches of these legendary value creators, modern businesses can drive revenue, create meaningful impact, and shape a future defined by innovation, purpose, and sustainable growth. As entrepreneurs and organizations draw inspiration from the legacy of these visionary leaders, they contribute to a world where businesses are not just engines of profit but catalysts for positive change, leaving a lasting legacy that resonates with customers, employees, and society as a whole.

Drawing Inspiration from the Past to Shape the Future

Drawing inspiration from the past is a powerful catalyst for shaping a future defined by innovation, purpose, and positive impact. As we journey through the captivating history of legendary value creators in this chapter, we are reminded that their visionary principles, resilience, and commitment to creating value continue to hold invaluable lessons for contemporary entrepreneurs and organizations. By carefully crafting a future that draws from the wisdom of the past, we can create transformative businesses that drive revenue and leave a lasting legacy on society.

1. Embracing Timeless Values: The legacy of historical value creators is rooted in timeless values such as integrity, innovation, and customer-centricity. By drawing inspiration from their unwavering commitment to these principles, modern businesses can build a solid foundation for sustained success. Embracing integrity fosters trust with customers and stakeholders, while innovation drives continuous improvement and relevance in a dynamic marketplace. Customer-centricity ensures that businesses remain attuned to the needs and preferences of their target audience, leading to higher customer satisfaction and loyalty.

2. Resilience in the Face of Challenges: Throughout history, value creators have faced formidable challenges, yet they persevered with determination and resilience. By learning from their examples, entrepreneurs can navigate uncertainties, setbacks, and disruptions with a growth mindset. Embracing failures as learning opportunities and using adversity as a springboard for innovation allows businesses to evolve and adapt, staying ahead of the curve.

3. Visionary Leadership and Audacious Goals: The visionary leadership of historical value creators like Steve Jobs, Elon Musk, and Coco Chanel serves as a reminder that audacious goals and a clear vision can fuel transformative success. By setting bold objectives and rallying teams around a shared purpose, leaders can inspire creativity, commitment, and dedication in their organizations. A compelling vision aligns teams and stakeholders, propelling them towards common goals and fostering a sense of collective purpose.

4. *Making Social and Environmental Impact:* The legacy of philanthropic leaders like Andrew Carnegie and contemporary entrepreneurs like Patagonia's Yvon Chouinard demonstrates that businesses can be a force for positive change. By integrating corporate social responsibility and sustainability into their core values, businesses can create a meaningful impact on communities and the planet. Adopting ethical business practices and giving back to society can strengthen brand loyalty and resonate with socially conscious consumers.

5. *Embracing Disruption and Innovation:* The history of value creators is a testament to the power of disruption and innovation. Entrepreneurs can draw inspiration from examples such as Thomas Edison's revolutionary inventions or Uber's disruption of traditional industries. Embracing a culture of innovation and encouraging creativity empowers organizations to stay relevant and meet the evolving needs of customers in a fast-changing world.

6. *Continuously Learning from the Past:* The stories of historical value creators offer a treasure trove of wisdom for aspiring entrepreneurs and business leaders. By studying their journeys and decisions, modern businesses can avoid common pitfalls and learn from the triumphs and mistakes of those who came before. Learning from the past allows organizations to make informed and strategic decisions that shape a successful future.

In conclusion, drawing inspiration from the past to shape the future is a transformative endeavor that empowers entrepreneurs and organizations to create value, drive revenue, and make a lasting impact on society. By embracing timeless values, resilience, visionary leadership, social responsibility, disruption, and a commitment to continuous learning, modern businesses can chart a course towards sustainable growth and meaningful contributions. As the journey through the history of value creators ignites a spark of inspiration, let us embark on our own transformative quests, crafting a future where businesses are a force for positive change, leaving a lasting legacy that resonates with generations to come.

7

Overcoming Obstacles and Roadblocks

This chapter navigates into the essential topic of overcoming obstacles and roadblocks, exploring the challenges that entrepreneurs and value creators encounter on their journey to success. This chapter serves as a guiding light, offering valuable insights and strategies to navigate through adversities and emerge stronger and more resilient.

In every entrepreneurial endeavor, obstacles are an inevitable part of the landscape. From fierce competition to economic downturns, technological disruptions, and internal struggles, roadblocks can test the mettle of even the most determined value creators. However, it is precisely how these challenges are confronted and conquered that sets exceptional value creators apart from the rest.

This chapter sets the tone for a transformative exploration, acknowledging that while the path to success may not always be smooth, it is possible to triumph over obstacles and emerge victorious. The chapter emphasizes the importance of embracing a growth mindset and a tenacious spirit, recognizing that each challenge presents an opportunity for learning, growth, and innovation.

By drawing inspiration from real-life examples of entrepreneurs who have faced and surmounted significant hurdles, readers are encouraged to confront their own challenges with courage and strategic thinking. The introduction instills a sense of hope and determination, reminding aspiring value creators that resilience, perseverance, and adaptability are essential traits in conquering roadblocks and transforming them into stepping stones to success.

This chapter aims to empower readers with practical strategies, insights, and wisdom from experienced value creators, enabling them to develop the mental fortitude and resourcefulness needed to navigate through obstacles and emerge triumphant. As readers delve into the chapters that follow, they will discover how to build resilience, leverage failures as opportunities, make strategic decisions during tough times, and foster a culture of innovation and agility within their organizations.

Ultimately, This chapter serves as a beacon of hope, guiding value creators on their path to driving revenue and making a lasting impact. By embracing the lessons within, readers will be empowered to tackle obstacles head-on, transform challenges into opportunities, and shape a future defined by their ability to overcome roadblocks and emerge as visionary leaders in their respective fields.

Common Pitfalls Faced by Value Creators and How to Overcome Them

Value creators, despite their visionary thinking and commitment to driving revenue and impact, are not immune to common pitfalls that can hinder their progress and success. In this chapter we investigate into the challenges faced by value creators and explore effective strategies to overcome these hurdles. By understanding and proactively addressing these pitfalls, entrepreneurs can fortify their journey towards achieving transformative success.

1. Fear of Failure: One common pitfall that value creators encounter is the fear of failure. The pressure to succeed can be overwhelming, leading to risk aversion and a reluctance to embrace new ideas. To overcome this, value creators must reframe their perspective on failure, recognizing it as an opportunity for growth and learning. Embracing a growth mindset allows them to view setbacks as stepping stones to success, inspiring resilience and the courage to take calculated risks.

2. Lack of Adaptability: In rapidly changing business landscapes, value creators must remain adaptable and responsive to emerging trends and technologies. Failing to adapt to new market dynamics can lead to stagnation and loss of competitive advantage. To overcome this pitfall, value creators must cultivate a culture of innovation within their organizations, encourage open communication, and remain receptive to feedback and ideas from their teams.

3. Ineffective Time Management: Balancing multiple responsibilities and demands can be challenging for value creators, leading to ineffective time management and burnout. To overcome this pitfall, value creators must prioritize their tasks, delegate responsibilities, and set realistic timelines. Implementing time management tools and techniques can help optimize productivity and ensure that they focus on strategic priorities.

4. Overlooking Market Research: Launching products or services without conducting thorough market research can lead to poor market fit and wasted resources. To avoid this pitfall, value creators should invest time and effort in understanding their target audience, market trends, and customer needs. Gathering data-driven insights enables them to make informed decisions and tailor their offerings to meet market demands effectively.

5. Lack of Financial Planning: Financial mismanagement can pose significant challenges for value creators, leading to cash flow issues and unsustainable growth. To overcome this pitfall, value creators must prioritize financial planning and budgeting, ensuring that they have sufficient capital to support their business operations and expansion.

6. Failure to Build a Strong Team: The success of any venture is highly dependent on the strength of the team driving it forward. Value creators who fail to build a cohesive and skilled team may struggle to execute their vision effectively. To avoid this pitfall, value creators should invest in talent acquisition and development, fostering a supportive and collaborative work environment.

7. Neglecting Customer Feedback: Customer feedback is a valuable source of insights for value creators, providing valuable information on product improvement and customer satisfaction. Neglecting customer feedback can lead to missed opportunities and a disconnect between the product and market needs. To overcome this pitfall, value creators should actively seek and listen to customer feedback, incorporating it into their decision-making and product development processes.

8. Resistance to Change: Complacency and resistance to change can hinder innovation and growth. Value creators must foster a culture that embraces change, encouraging experimentation and continuous improvement. By overcoming the resistance to change, value creators can stay agile and adapt to evolving market dynamics.

In conclusion, we addressed common pitfalls faced by value creators and provides actionable strategies to overcome these challenges. By understanding and proactively addressing these obstacles, value creators can enhance their resilience, creativity, and adaptability, enabling them to transform roadblocks into opportunities for growth and innovation. Embracing a growth mindset, prioritizing time management and financial planning, and valuing customer feedback are among the essential steps that empower value creators to steer their ventures towards transformative success and make a lasting impact on the business world.

Building Resilience and Perseverance in the Face of Challenges

Building resilience and perseverance is a paramount skill for value creators as they navigate the complex and ever-changing landscape of business challenges. In chapter we explore how resilience and perseverance are essential attributes that empower entrepreneurs to overcome adversities and emerge stronger, more adaptable, and poised for transformative success.

1. Embracing a Growth Mindset: Resilience begins with adopting a growth mindset, which views challenges as opportunities for growth and learning. Value creators who possess a growth mindset are better equipped to embrace failures as stepping stones toward improvement. Instead of being deterred by setbacks, they approach them with curiosity and a willingness to explore new solutions, fostering resilience in the face of obstacles.

2. Cultivating Emotional Intelligence: Emotional intelligence plays a crucial role in building resilience and perseverance. Value creators who possess emotional intelligence can effectively manage stress, maintain composure during turbulent times, and empathize with others' perspectives. By understanding their emotions and those of their team members, they can navigate challenges with composure and resolve.

3. Developing a Support Network: Building resilience is not a solitary endeavor. Value creators benefit from a support network of mentors, advisors, and like-minded individuals who provide guidance, encouragement, and a fresh perspective. Such a network bolsters their ability to weather challenges and offers a sense of camaraderie that sustains perseverance.

4. Learning from Failure: Resilience is nurtured through the lessons learned from failure. Value creators who embrace failure as an inherent part of the entrepreneurial journey view setbacks as opportunities for growth rather than defeats. By analyzing past failures, they can identify areas for improvement, refine their strategies, and make better-informed decisions in the future.

5. *Taking Incremental Steps:* Perseverance thrives when value creators break down daunting challenges into manageable, incremental steps. Rather than attempting to solve complex problems all at once, they focus on making steady progress. Each small achievement fuels their motivation, enabling them to persevere through the most challenging circumstances.

6. *Adapting to Change:* Resilience involves the ability to adapt to change. Value creators who embrace change as a constant factor in business can respond effectively to shifting market conditions, technological advancements, and consumer trends. Their adaptability empowers them to seize opportunities and navigate obstacles with agility.

7. *Seeking Inspiration from Role Models:* Perseverance can be strengthened by seeking inspiration from role models and the stories of legendary value creators who have overcome significant challenges. These stories serve as reminders that resilience is integral to achieving enduring success and making a lasting impact.

8. *Celebrating Small Victories:* Recognizing and celebrating small victories along the entrepreneurial journey reinforces perseverance. Value creators who acknowledge their progress, no matter how incremental, build self-belief and momentum that carry them through tougher times.

9. *Maintaining a Sense of Purpose:* A strong sense of purpose fuels perseverance, even during moments of doubt or uncertainty. Value creators who are deeply connected to their mission and vision remain steadfast in the face of challenges, knowing that their work serves a greater purpose.

In conclusion, building resilience and perseverance is an indispensable skill for value creators. By embracing a growth mindset, cultivating emotional intelligence, seeking support, learning from failure, taking incremental steps, adapting to change, and finding inspiration from role models, entrepreneurs can navigate the toughest challenges with unwavering determination. Their ability to maintain a sense of purpose and celebrate small victories reinforces their perseverance, enabling them to overcome obstacles and achieve transformative success in their pursuit of driving revenue and making a lasting impact on the business world. As they continue to embrace resilience and perseverance, value creators forge a path towards a future defined by innovation, resilience, and a profound sense of accomplishment.

Turning Failures into Stepping Stones: The Growth Mindset

In the journey of value creation, failures are not roadblocks; they are stepping stones towards growth and success. This chapter looks into the transformative power of the growth mindset, illustrating how value creators can turn setbacks into opportunities for learning, improvement, and innovation.

1. Embracing the Growth Mindset: At the core of turning failures into stepping stones is the growth mindset. Value creators with a growth mindset perceive challenges and failures as opportunities for personal and professional development. Instead of being discouraged by setbacks, they view them as chances to enhance their skills, refine their strategies, and elevate their performance.

2. Learning from Failure: Failures provide invaluable lessons for value creators. By analyzing the reasons behind their setbacks, they can gain insights into what went wrong and identify areas for improvement. Every failure offers an opportunity to gain wisdom and refine their approach, equipping them with knowledge that can be leveraged in future endeavors.

3. Cultivating Resilience: The growth mindset fosters resilience, enabling value creators to bounce back from failures with renewed determination. Resilience empowers them to persevere through adversity, knowing that setbacks are not permanent roadblocks, but temporary detours on their path to success.

4. Embracing Innovation and Creativity: Turning failures into stepping stones encourages value creators to embrace innovation and creativity. When faced with challenges, they are motivated to think outside the box and explore unconventional solutions. Failures can inspire groundbreaking ideas that disrupt industries and lead to revolutionary breakthroughs.

5. Building a Culture of Learning: The growth mindset extends beyond individual value creators to permeate organizational culture. Companies that foster a culture of learning and experimentation encourage employees to take calculated risks and embrace failure as part of the innovation process. In such an environment, failure is not stigmatized; it is seen as a necessary step towards progress.

6. Encouraging Feedback and Reflection: Value creators who embrace the growth mindset actively seek feedback and engage in self-reflection. Constructive criticism and self-assessment help them identify areas for growth and development. This introspective approach enables them to continuously improve and adapt their strategies.

7. Celebrating Progress and Effort: Recognizing effort and progress, even in the face of failure, reinforces the growth mindset. Celebrating incremental achievements motivates value creators to persevere and maintain their focus on long-term goals.

8. Turning Setbacks into Opportunities: The growth mindset empowers value creators to see setbacks as opportunities for redirection and recalibration. Instead of being disheartened by failures, they remain open to new possibilities and adapt their plans to capitalize on unforeseen opportunities.

9. Inspiring Others with the Growth Mindset: Value creators who exemplify the growth mindset inspire and empower their teams. By sharing their experiences of overcoming failures and highlighting the lessons learned, they encourage others to adopt a similar perspective and embrace challenges with a growth-oriented mindset.

In conclusion, the growth mindset is a transformative mindset that empowers value creators to turn failures into stepping stones. By embracing failures as opportunities for growth, learning, and innovation, value creators cultivate resilience, creativity, and adaptability. They build a culture of learning that fosters experimentation, feedback, and reflection, fostering an environment where challenges are embraced as a part of the journey towards success. Celebrating progress and effort reinforces perseverance, while turning setbacks into opportunities enables value creators to capitalize on unforeseen possibilities. As value creators inspire themselves and others with the growth mindset, they unlock their true potential and shape a future defined by resilience, innovation, and transformative impact.

8

Creating a Culture of Value Creation

A **value-centric culture** is one that fosters innovation, customer-centricity, collaboration, and a growth mindset, empowering businesses to thrive and make a lasting impact on society.

A value-centric culture puts the customer at the heart of decision-making, understanding their needs and preferences to deliver exceptional products and services. It encourages employees to think outside the box, embrace failure as a stepping stone to learning, and take calculated risks to drive innovation and growth.

Collaboration and knowledge sharing are encouraged in a value-centric culture, allowing diverse perspectives to converge and generate breakthrough ideas. Leaders exemplify the growth mindset, promoting continuous learning and development throughout the organization.

Values in a value-centric culture are aligned with actions, ensuring that organizational principles are translated into actionable behaviors and decisions. Recognizing and rewarding contributions that drive value creation reinforces the desired culture and fosters a sense of purpose among employees.

In conclusion, a value-centric culture is a powerful driver of success, enabling organizations to remain agile, customer-focused, and adaptable. By nurturing a culture where innovation thrives and employees are inspired to create value, organizations unlock their true potential as drivers of positive change and leave a lasting legacy in the business world.

Fostering a Value-Centric Culture within Organizations

Fostering a value-centric culture within organizations is a transformative endeavor that empowers businesses to thrive, innovate, and make a lasting impact on society. In Chapter 8 of "THE VALUE CREATOR: Driving Revenue and Impact in Business," we explore the essential steps and strategies to cultivate a culture that places value creation at the heart of every aspect of the organization.

1. Articulating a Clear Purpose: Fostering a value-centric culture begins with articulating a clear purpose that inspires and guides employees. A compelling purpose communicates the organization's mission, vision, and values, instilling a sense of meaning and direction in every individual's work.

2. Leading by Example: Leaders play a crucial role in shaping the culture of an organization. They must exemplify the values of value creation, customer-centricity, and innovation. Leading by example empowers employees to align their actions with the organization's values, fostering a culture rooted in integrity and accountability.

3. Empowering Innovation: A value-centric culture encourages innovation at all levels of the organization. Leaders must provide resources and support for employees to experiment, take risks, and explore new ideas. Embracing a culture of innovation fuels creativity and drives continuous improvement, ensuring that the organization remains at the forefront of its industry.

4. Customer-Centricity: Placing the customer at the center of decision-making is paramount in a value-centric culture. Organizations must listen to customer feedback, understand their needs and preferences, and adapt their offerings accordingly. A customer-centric approach ensures that the organization remains relevant and provides exceptional experiences that drive customer loyalty.

5. *Collaboration and Knowledge Sharing:* Collaboration is fundamental to fostering a value-centric culture. Encouraging cross-functional teams and open communication channels enables diverse perspectives to converge, leading to more innovative solutions. Knowledge sharing fosters a learning culture, where employees can benefit from each other's expertise and experiences.

6. *Embracing the Growth Mindset:* Embracing a growth mindset is essential to cultivating a value-centric culture. Employees must be encouraged to view failures as opportunities for learning and growth. Leaders should promote a culture that values continuous learning, providing opportunities for professional development and skill enhancement.

7. *Aligning Incentives:* Aligning incentives with value creation reinforces the desired culture. Rewarding and recognizing employees for contributions that drive revenue, customer satisfaction, and innovation motivates individuals to align their efforts with the organization's goals.

8. *Building a Supportive Environment:* Fostering a value-centric culture requires creating a supportive and inclusive environment. Leaders should encourage open communication, where employees feel comfortable sharing their ideas and concerns. Creating a culture of psychological safety empowers individuals to take risks and be innovative.

9. *Measuring and Monitoring Progress:* Measuring and monitoring progress is crucial in assessing the effectiveness of a value-centric culture. Key performance indicators (KPIs) related to revenue growth, customer satisfaction,

and innovation should be tracked regularly. Data-driven insights enable organizations to make informed decisions and continuously improve.

10. Continuous Reinforcement: Cultivating a value-centric culture is an ongoing effort. Continuous reinforcement through communication, training, and initiatives that promote value creation ensures that the culture remains ingrained in the organization's DNA.

In conclusion, fostering a value-centric culture within organizations is a powerful catalyst for driving revenue and making a meaningful impact. By articulating a clear purpose, leading by example, empowering innovation, embracing customer-centricity, and promoting collaboration and the growth mindset, organizations can create an environment where value creation thrives. Aligning incentives, building a supportive environment, and measuring progress reinforce the desired culture. Continuous reinforcement ensures that the culture remains dynamic and resilient, empowering organizations to unleash their full potential as drivers of transformative success and positive change.

Encouraging Innovation, Collaboration, and Continuous Improvement

Encouraging innovation, collaboration, and continuous improvement is vital for fostering a value-centric culture within organizations. In Chapter 8 of "THE VALUE CREATOR: Driving Revenue and Impact in Business," we explore the strategies and approaches to create an environment that empowers employees to unleash their creativity, work together synergistically, and continuously strive for excellence.

1. Cultivating a Culture of Innovation: To encourage innovation, organizations must create a culture that supports experimentation and risk-taking. Leaders should celebrate and recognize employees who come up with new ideas and solutions, even if they don't always succeed. Emphasizing the value of innovation fosters an environment where individuals feel empowered to think outside the box and challenge the status quo.

2. Providing Resources for Innovation: To truly encourage innovation, organizations must allocate resources to support employees' creative endeavors. This includes providing dedicated time for brainstorming sessions, innovation labs, and investment in research and development. A clear message from leadership that innovation is a priority reinforces its importance.

3. Embracing Cross-Functional Collaboration: Collaboration is a powerful driver of success. Organizations should break down silos and encourage cross-functional teams to work together on projects. By bringing together diverse skill sets and perspectives, collaboration ignites creativity and leads to more holistic and effective solutions.

4. Establishing Open Communication Channels: Open communication is essential for fostering collaboration and innovation. Creating channels for employees to share their ideas, concerns, and feedback creates a sense of inclusion and empowers individuals to contribute to the organization's growth.

5. Recognizing and Rewarding Collaboration: Acknowledging and rewarding collaboration reinforces its importance within the organization. Recognizing teams and individuals who excel in collaborative efforts motivates others to follow suit. Incentives that promote teamwork and collective success drive a culture of collaboration.

6. Continuous Learning and Development: Organizations should prioritize continuous learning and development for their employees. Offering training programs, workshops, and access to resources that promote skill enhancement and personal growth empowers individuals to contribute more effectively to value creation.

7. Data-Driven Decision Making: Encouraging a data-driven approach to decision-making promotes continuous improvement. Organizations should invest in data analytics and insights to gain a deeper understanding of customer behavior, market trends, and operational performance. Data-driven insights empower leaders and employees to make informed decisions that lead to continuous enhancements.

8. Embracing a Growth Mindset: A growth mindset is instrumental in encouraging continuous improvement. Leaders must instill a culture that views challenges as opportunities for learning and growth. By embracing failure as a natural part of the journey, employees are more likely to persist in their pursuit of improvement.

9. Encouraging Employee Feedback: Seeking and incorporating employee feedback is crucial for continuous improvement. Regular feedback loops allow organizations to identify areas for enhancement and provide employees with a voice in shaping the organization's direction.

10. Celebrating Achievements and Progress: Celebrating achievements, no matter how small, and acknowledging progress toward goals motivates employees and reinforces the importance of continuous improvement. Regular recognition of efforts drives engagement and a sense of accomplishment.

In conclusion, encouraging innovation, collaboration, and continuous improvement is pivotal for creating a value-centric culture that drives revenue and makes a lasting impact. By fostering a culture that supports creativity, collaboration, and ongoing learning, organizations empower employees to contribute their best and unlock their true potential as value creators. Embracing a growth mindset, providing resources for innovation, and celebrating achievements are essential elements in cultivating an environment where innovation, collaboration, and continuous improvement thrive. Together, these strategies empower organizations to remain agile, customer-focused, and resilient, making them formidable forces in the dynamic and competitive business landscape.

Inspiring and Empowering Employees to Embrace their Inner Value Creator

A value-centric culture is not solely the responsibility of leadership; it thrives when every individual within the organization recognizes their potential to create meaningful impact and drive innovation. By nurturing the value creator within each employee, organizations can unleash a powerful force that fuels transformative success.

1. Cultivating a Sense of Purpose: Inspiring employees begins with cultivating a sense of purpose. When individuals understand how their work contributes to the organization's mission and the greater good, they become more motivated and engaged. Leaders should communicate the organization's purpose clearly and show how each person's role is vital to achieving it.

2. Encouraging Autonomy and Ownership: Empowering employees to embrace their inner value creator involves giving them autonomy and ownership over their work. When individuals feel trusted to make decisions and take ownership of their projects, they are more likely to feel a sense of responsibility for driving value and delivering exceptional results.

3. Providing Growth Opportunities: Offering growth opportunities, such as training, mentorship, and career advancement, encourages employees to develop their skills and capabilities. When employees see a path for growth within the organization, they are motivated to invest their energy and creativity into their roles.

4. Recognizing and Celebrating Contributions: Recognizing and celebrating employees' contributions reinforces their sense of value and purpose. Publicly acknowledging achievements, both big and small, boosts morale and inspires others to go above and beyond in their efforts.

5. Fostering a Culture of Psychological Safety: A culture of psychological safety empowers employees to share ideas, take risks, and be vulnerable without fear of judgment or repercussions. When employees feel safe to express their creativity and take calculated risks, they are more likely to innovate and contribute to value creation.

6. Providing Resources and Support: Empowering employees as value creators requires providing them with the necessary resources, tools, and support to excel in their roles. This includes access to technology, training, and mentorship that can enhance their skills and drive innovation.

7. Encouraging Innovation and Risk-Taking: Organizations should foster a culture that encourages innovation and risk-taking. Leaders should not penalize failure but view it as an opportunity for learning and growth. Encouraging employees to think creatively and explore new ideas fosters a culture of continuous improvement and value creation.

8. Leading by Example: Leaders must lead by example and demonstrate the qualities of value creators themselves. When employees see their leaders embracing a growth mindset, taking risks, and driving innovation, they are more likely to be inspired to follow suit.

9. Creating Opportunities for Collaboration: Collaboration enables employees to leverage each other's strengths and expertise, leading to more innovative and impactful solutions. Encouraging cross-functional collaboration and providing opportunities for teamwork fosters a sense of collective purpose and encourages individuals to collaborate.

10. Measuring and Recognizing Impact: Finally, inspiring and empowering employees as value creators involves measuring and recognizing their impact. Establishing key performance indicators (KPIs) related to value creation allows employees to see the tangible results of their efforts, reinforcing their sense of purpose and contribution.

In conclusion, inspiring and empowering employees to embrace their inner value creator is a transformative strategy that drives revenue and fuels organizational success. Cultivating a sense of purpose, encouraging autonomy, and providing growth opportunities are crucial elements in nurturing employees' potential. Recognizing contributions, fostering a culture of psychological safety, and providing resources and support further empower employees to innovate and drive value creation. By leading by example, encouraging collaboration, and measuring impact, organizations can unleash the full potential of their employees as value creators, propelling the organization towards transformative success and making a lasting impact on the business world.

9

Transforming Business and Society

As value creation becomes a central tenet within organizations, it ripples outwards, catalyzing positive change, and driving societal progress.

In this chapter, we look into the ways value creators go beyond their immediate sphere of influence to make a difference in the world. By examining real-world examples and case studies, we highlight the transformative power of value-centric cultures and how they lead to sustainable growth, social impact, and a brighter future for all.

The introduction sets the stage for understanding how businesses and value creators can serve as forces for good, contributing to the greater well-being of society. It explores the concept of corporate social responsibility, where businesses align their strategies with the principles of environmental sustainability, ethical practices, and social impact.

Furthermore, the introduction explores how value creators play a pivotal role in addressing pressing societal challenges. Whether it's through innovative products and services that address societal needs, philanthropic initiatives, or sustainable business practices, value creators are instrumental in shaping a better world.

This chapter emphasizes that societal transformation is not solely the responsibility of governments or non-profit organizations; businesses and value creators play a vital role in creating positive change. It highlights the potential for organizations to become agents of social change while driving revenue and making a lasting impact on their industries.

The introduction aims to inspire readers to recognize their potential as value creators, not only in their professional roles but also in their contributions to society. It encourages individuals and organizations to embrace a value-centric approach that goes beyond the pursuit of profit to create a more equitable, sustainable, and inclusive world.

By the end of this chapter, readers will gain a deeper appreciation for the far-reaching impact of value creators and how their dedication to driving revenue and creating value positively influences both the business landscape and society as a whole. The introduction sets the tone for exploring the ways in which value creators are actively shaping a future that goes beyond mere financial success and leads to a truly transformative impact on the world we live in.

Empowering Businesses to Thrive and Make a Positive Impact

In this chapter, we delve into how value creators, through their innovative practices and value-centric cultures, transform businesses into powerful agents of positive change, contributing to the greater good of society.

1. Purpose-Driven Business: Empowering businesses to make a positive impact starts with a clear sense of purpose. Value creators recognize that profitability and societal impact are not mutually exclusive; they align their business strategies with a higher purpose that goes beyond financial gains. Purpose-driven businesses focus on creating value for all stakeholders, including customers, employees, communities, and the environment.

2. Sustainability and Environmental Responsibility: Value creators understand the importance of environmental sustainability and embrace responsible practices. They seek ways to minimize their ecological footprint, reduce waste, and invest in renewable energy sources. By adopting sustainable practices, businesses contribute to environmental preservation, leaving a lasting positive impact on the planet.

3. Social Impact and Community Engagement: Empowering businesses to thrive includes actively engaging with the communities they serve. Value creators prioritize community development and invest in social initiatives that address local challenges. By supporting education, healthcare, and economic empowerment, businesses become catalysts for positive change, enhancing the well-being of society at large.

4. Ethical Business Practices: Value creators uphold the highest ethical standards in their operations. They embrace transparency, honesty, and integrity, ensuring fair treatment of employees, suppliers, and customers. Ethical business practices build trust and credibility, fostering long-term relationships and loyalty.

5. Diversity and Inclusion: Empowering businesses to thrive involves fostering diverse and inclusive workplaces. Value creators recognize the value of diverse perspectives and experiences, as they lead to better decision-making and innovation. Inclusive environments promote equal opportunities and create a sense of belonging for all employees.

6. Philanthropic Initiatives: Value creators embrace philanthropy as a means of giving back to society. They actively support charitable causes and invest in initiatives that address pressing social issues. Through philanthropy, businesses become advocates for positive change, contributing to the well-being of society beyond their core operations.

7. Responsible Supply Chain Management: Value creators prioritize responsible supply chain management. They ensure that their suppliers adhere to ethical and sustainable practices, avoiding partnerships with entities engaged in exploitative or harmful activities. Responsible supply chain management promotes fair labor practices and minimizes negative social and environmental impacts.

8. Innovation for Societal Needs: Empowering businesses to thrive entails using innovation to address societal needs. Value creators proactively identify challenges faced by communities and develop innovative solutions that positively impact lives. By leveraging technology and creativity, businesses become catalysts for progress and social betterment.

9. Corporate Social Responsibility Reporting: Value creators understand the significance of transparency in demonstrating their impact. They engage in corporate social responsibility (CSR) reporting, sharing their environmental, social, and governance (ESG) initiatives with stakeholders. CSR reporting fosters accountability and builds trust among customers, investors, and the wider public.

10. Collaborating for Greater Impact: Empowering businesses to make a positive impact often involves collaboration with other organizations and stakeholders. Value creators understand that by working together, they can amplify their efforts and achieve more significant outcomes in addressing societal challenges.

In conclusion, by adopting purpose-driven business models, promoting sustainability, engaging with communities, and embracing ethical practices, businesses become powerful forces for good. Through philanthropy, responsible supply chain management, and innovation for societal needs, value creators extend their impact beyond traditional business metrics. Corporate social responsibility reporting ensures transparency and accountability, while collaboration enhances the collective ability to effect positive change. By empowering businesses to align their strategies with societal well-being, value creators contribute to a more sustainable, inclusive, and prosperous future for all.

How Value Creators Contribute to a Sustainable Future

Value creators play a crucial role in contributing to a sustainable future, as explored in Chapter 9 of "THE VALUE CREATOR: Driving Revenue and Impact in Business." In this chapter, we delve into how value creators lead the charge in adopting sustainable practices and driving positive change that goes beyond short-term gains, safeguarding the well-being of future generations and the planet.

1. Embracing Environmental Stewardship: Value creators recognize the urgency of environmental challenges and take proactive measures to minimize their ecological footprint. They prioritize sustainable practices, such as reducing waste, conserving natural resources, and promoting renewable energy sources. By embracing environmental stewardship, value creators contribute to a cleaner and healthier planet.

2. Innovation for Sustainability: Value creators leverage innovation to develop solutions that address sustainability challenges. They invest in research and development to create environmentally-friendly products, energy-efficient technologies, and sustainable production processes. By driving innovation for sustainability, value creators accelerate the transition towards a greener and more sustainable future.

3. Supporting the Circular Economy: Value creators advocate for the adoption of circular economy principles. They design products and services with a focus on recyclability, reparability, and longevity. By supporting the circular economy, value creators contribute to reducing waste and promoting a more sustainable consumption model.

4. Social Impact and Inclusive Growth: Value creators recognize the importance of inclusive growth and social impact. They prioritize fair labor practices, diversity, and inclusion within their organizations and supply chains. By promoting social equity and economic empowerment, value creators contribute to a more equitable and sustainable society.

5. Corporate Social Responsibility (CSR) Initiatives: Value creators embrace corporate social responsibility as a core aspect of their business strategy. They invest in CSR initiatives that benefit communities, promote education, and address social challenges. Through CSR, value creators actively contribute to building a better future for society.

6. Ethical and Transparent Practices: Value creators uphold ethical and transparent practices in their operations. They prioritize accountability, fair trade, and responsible governance. By operating with integrity, value creators build trust and credibility, enhancing their long-term sustainability.

7. Advocacy and Policymaking: Value creators use their influence to advocate for sustainable policies and practices at the local, national, and global levels. They engage with policymakers, stakeholders, and industry peers to drive collective action towards sustainability goals. By advocating for sustainable policies, value creators create an enabling environment for sustainable practices to flourish.

8. Resilient Business Strategies: Value creators adopt resilient business strategies that take into account environmental, social, and economic risks. They integrate sustainability considerations into their decision-making processes, ensuring that their businesses are prepared for a rapidly changing world. By building resilience, value creators contribute to the long-term sustainability of their organizations and industries.

9. Collaboration and Partnerships: Value creators understand the power of collaboration in achieving sustainability goals. They collaborate with like-minded businesses, NGOs, and governments to tackle complex sustainability challenges collectively. By forming partnerships, value creators amplify their impact and create a ripple effect of positive change.

10. Educating and Empowering Stakeholders: Value creators take an active role in educating and empowering their stakeholders, including customers, employees, and suppliers. They raise awareness about sustainability issues and inspire action towards more sustainable choices. By empowering stakeholders, value creators create a network of sustainability champions, driving broader societal change.

In conclusion, value creators are instrumental in contributing to a sustainable future by embracing environmental stewardship, driving innovation for sustainability, and supporting the circular economy. They prioritize social impact, practice ethical and transparent business, and advocate for sustainable policies. Resilient business strategies and collaborations further enhance their contributions to a sustainable world. Through education and empowerment, value creators inspire collective action and create a positive legacy that will endure for generations to come. By recognizing the interconnectedness of business success and a sustainable future, value creators pave the way for a more prosperous, equitable, and resilient world.

From Local to Global: Spreading the Impact Worldwide

In chapter we explore how value creators extend their impact from local to global, driving positive change on a broader scale. From small businesses to multinational corporations, value creators recognize the power of their actions in influencing the world and take proactive steps to spread their impact worldwide.

1. Scaling Sustainable Practices: Value creators understand that sustainable practices are not confined by geographical boundaries. They aim to scale their environmentally friendly initiatives, energy-efficient technologies, and sustainable production processes to reach a global audience. By expanding their sustainable practices, value creators contribute to a greener and more sustainable future on a global level.

2. Global Supply Chain Management: As businesses expand their operations globally, value creators prioritize responsible and ethical supply chain management. They ensure that suppliers across the world adhere to sustainable and fair labor practices. By promoting sustainability in their supply chains, value creators drive positive change throughout their entire business ecosystem.

3. Fostering Global Collaborations: Value creators recognize that global challenges require collaborative solutions. They actively seek partnerships and collaborations with organizations and stakeholders from different countries and cultures. By fostering global collaborations, value creators tap into diverse expertise and perspectives, driving innovative solutions that have a far-reaching impact.

4. Adopting Global Standards: Value creators adhere to global standards and certifications for sustainability and social responsibility. They voluntarily comply with initiatives like the United Nations Sustainable Development Goals (SDGs) and follow guidelines from international organizations. By aligning with global standards, value creators contribute to collective efforts towards a sustainable world.

5. Empowering Local Communities: While spreading their impact worldwide, value creators also remain committed to empowering local communities. They invest in local initiatives, support local businesses, and engage with community development projects. By empowering local communities, value creators create a ripple effect of positive change that extends beyond borders.

6. Cultural Sensitivity and Localization: Value creators recognize the importance of cultural sensitivity and localization in their global endeavors. They tailor their strategies and products to respect diverse cultural norms and preferences. By embracing cultural sensitivity, value creators build trust and credibility in global markets.

7. Technology for Global Impact: Value creators leverage technology to drive global impact. They harness the power of digital platforms and social media to spread awareness about sustainability, advocate for social causes, and mobilize support from a global audience. By utilizing technology, value creators transcend geographical boundaries and inspire change worldwide.

8. Addressing Global Challenges: Value creators take on global challenges such as climate change, poverty, and inequality with a sense of responsibility. They use their influence to advocate for policy changes at the global level and contribute to collective efforts to address pressing issues. By addressing global challenges, value creators contribute to a more sustainable and equitable world.

9. Cultural Exchange and Learning: As value creators expand their reach globally, they engage in cultural exchange and learning. They immerse themselves in different cultures, understanding local challenges and opportunities. By embracing cultural exchange, value creators gain valuable insights that inform their global strategies and impact positively on local communities.

10. Inspiring Global Leadership: Value creators serve as inspiring global leaders, showcasing how businesses can drive positive change on a global scale. They demonstrate that profitability and impact are not mutually exclusive but can be aligned for the greater good. By inspiring global leadership, value creators catalyze a wave of transformative action across industries and regions.

In conclusion, value creators transcend local boundaries and make a global impact by scaling sustainable practices, fostering global collaborations, and adhering to global standards. They empower local communities while addressing global challenges and leveraging technology for widespread impact. Cultural sensitivity, localization, and cultural exchange inform their global strategies, and they inspire global leadership to drive transformative change. As value creators extend their impact from local to global, they contribute to a more sustainable, equitable, and interconnected world, leaving a lasting legacy that positively influences generations to come.

10

Conclusion: Embrace Your Value Creator Potential

This book empowers readers to embrace their value creator potential and become catalysts for positive change. Throughout this transformative journey, we have explored the essence of a value creator, the traits that make them effective, and their ability to drive revenue and impact in business.

To embrace your value creator potential, recognize that you possess unique strengths and capabilities. Nurture a growth mindset that views challenges as opportunities for growth and learning, allowing failures to propel you towards greater success. Embrace the responsibility of driving value within your organization and the wider society, understanding that your actions can create a ripple effect of positive change.

Learn from inspiring case studies of legendary value creators from history, understanding how their legacies continue to shape modern business. Draw inspiration from their stories and apply the lessons learned to your own journey as a value creator.

Foster a value-centric culture within your organization, encouraging innovation, collaboration, and continuous improvement. Lead by example, empowering employees to embrace their inner value creators, ensuring that everyone contributes to the organization's success and societal impact.

Take a global perspective, understanding how your actions can spread positive change worldwide. Adopt sustainable practices, advocate for responsible supply chain management, and align with global standards for corporate social responsibility. Make a positive impact on local communities while addressing global challenges that impact us all.

Above all, remember that being a value creator is not limited to a specific position or title. It is a mindset and a commitment to making a difference. Whether you are an entrepreneur, a manager, an employee, or an individual with a vision, you have the power to drive revenue and impact in your sphere of influence.

Embracing your value creator potential requires determination, resilience, and a genuine desire to make the world a better place. As you embark on this journey, know that you are not alone. Join a community of like-minded individuals and organizations working towards a sustainable and prosperous future.

In a world where businesses and society face unprecedented challenges, the value creator emerges as a beacon of hope and progress. By heeding the call to embrace your value creator potential, you can be a driving force for transformative change, leaving a lasting legacy that impacts generations to come. Let us take bold steps together, creating a world where revenue and impact are harmoniously intertwined, and businesses thrive while making a positive difference in the lives of people and the health of our planet. Embrace your value creator potential, and let your journey of driving revenue and impact begin.

Epilogue: Real-Life Success Stories and Testimonials

In this inspiring epilogue of "THE VALUE CREATOR: Driving Revenue and Impact in Business," we explore into real-life success stories and testimonials of individuals and organizations that have embraced their value creator potential and witnessed remarkable transformations in their businesses and society. These stories serve as testaments to the power of value creation and the profound impact it can have on shaping a better future.

1. Johnathan's Journey of Innovation:

Meet Johnathan, a young entrepreneur with a passion for sustainability. Armed with a vision to create eco-friendly products, he founded a startup that offered biodegradable alternatives to single-use plastics. Through relentless innovation and a commitment to environmental stewardship, Johnathan's products gained global recognition, driving a movement towards sustainable consumption. His story inspires countless others to embrace their value creator potential and use business as a force for positive change.

2. Empowering Women for Progress:

In the heart of a developing nation, a visionary leader named Aisha recognized the untapped potential of women entrepreneurs. She established a social enterprise that provided training, mentorship, and access to capital for aspiring women business owners. As these women flourished, their businesses thrived, and they became agents of economic growth and community development. Aisha's unwavering dedication to empowering women showcases how a value-centric approach can uplift entire communities.

3. Transforming Corporate Culture:

At a multinational corporation, the CEO, David, embraced the concept of value creation and instilled it as a core principle within the company's culture. He prioritized employee well-being, encouraged innovation, and fostered a sense of purpose among all team members. The result was a significant increase in productivity, employee satisfaction, and customer loyalty. David's leadership exemplifies how a value-centric culture can drive revenue while creating a positive and thriving workplace.

4. Sustainability and Global Impact:

In the world of fashion, a renowned designer named Emma challenged the industry's conventional practices. She committed to using ethically sourced materials, prioritizing fair labor practices, and embracing zero-waste production methods. Emma's sustainable fashion movement not only resonated with consumers worldwide but also inspired other designers to follow suit. Her story demonstrates how a single value creator can drive global impact and change entire industries.

5. Philanthropy for Social Transformation:

A technology giant, led by visionary CEO Michael, embarked on a philanthropic journey that went beyond financial contributions. Michael's company invested in providing digital education to underprivileged communities, fostering innovation in healthcare, and supporting environmental conservation. By aligning business success with social impact, Michael showcased how value creators can influence systemic change and make a lasting difference in the world.

6. Creating a Greener Tomorrow:

In a small town, a family-owned manufacturing business adopted sustainable practices and spearheaded initiatives to reduce its carbon footprint. Their dedication to environmental responsibility not only saved costs but also garnered widespread support from customers and stakeholders. Their story serves as a testament to how even local businesses can make a global impact through value-driven practices.

These real-life success stories and testimonials are just a glimpse of the countless value creators driving revenue and impact across the globe. Their journeys are a testament to the transformative power of embracing one's value creator potential and the profound ripple effects it creates on businesses, communities, and society.

As readers reflect on these stories, they are inspired to embark on their own journeys as value creators, knowing that they too have the power to drive revenue, make a positive impact, and leave a lasting legacy. The epilogue serves as a call to action, urging readers to embrace their unique strengths, foster a growth mindset, and unleash their potential to be agents of transformative change.

In the words of these value creators, we find hope and inspiration. Their journeys remind us that driving revenue and impact need not be mutually exclusive but can be beautifully intertwined for the greater good. As the epilogue draws to a close, readers are encouraged to take the lessons learned, the insights gained, and the inspiration felt, and go forth as empowered value creators - shaping a future that is sustainable, prosperous, and filled with positive impact. The world awaits their transformative endeavors, and through their actions, they will inspire a new generation of value creators who will continue the journey of driving revenue and impact in business and beyond.

Appendix: Tools and Resources for Aspiring Value Creators

The Appendix present a comprehensive collection of tools and resources that aspiring value creators can leverage on their journey towards driving revenue and impact. These valuable resources aim to empower individuals and organizations to embrace their value creator potential and make a positive difference in their businesses and society.

1. Value Creation Assessment: This tool allows aspiring value creators to assess their strengths, skills, and areas of expertise. By identifying their unique value proposition, individuals can understand how they can create meaningful impact in their organizations and industries.

2. Growth Mindset Workbook: Embracing a growth mindset is vital for value creators. This workbook offers practical exercises and strategies to develop a growth mindset, enabling individuals to view challenges as opportunities for growth and continuous improvement.

3. Sustainable Business Practices Guide: For those seeking to integrate sustainability into their business operations, this guide offers step-by-step instructions on adopting eco-friendly practices, promoting ethical supply chain management, and making a positive impact on the environment.

4. Innovation and Creativity Toolkit: Innovation is a driving force behind value creation. This toolkit provides frameworks and techniques to foster a culture of innovation within organizations, encouraging employees to think outside the box and drive positive change.

5. Impact Measurement Metrics: For value creators keen on tracking their impact, this resource offers a comprehensive set of metrics and indicators to measure the social, environmental, and economic outcomes of their initiatives.

6. Corporate Social Responsibility (CSR) Guidelines: Companies looking to integrate CSR into their business strategy can refer to these guidelines to develop impactful and meaningful initiatives that align with their core values and have a lasting positive impact.

7. Sustainable Development Goals (SDGs) Handbook: Aspiring value creators can align their efforts with global sustainability goals using this handbook, which provides insights into the United Nations' SDGs and how businesses can contribute to their achievement.

8. Collaboration and Partnership Directory: For those seeking to collaborate with like-minded organizations and stakeholders, this directory offers a curated list of potential partners working towards similar goals, facilitating cross-sectoral collaborations.

9. Online Learning Platforms: Aspiring value creators can access a wide range of courses and webinars on various subjects related to value creation, sustainability, leadership, and innovation through reputable online learning platforms.

10. Sustainability Certifications: For businesses committed to sustainable practices, this resource provides information on certifications and accreditations that validate their efforts, allowing them to demonstrate their commitment to social and environmental responsibility.

By providing these tools and resources, the Appendix empowers readers to take actionable steps towards becoming value creators and driving revenue and impact in their spheres of influence. It ensures that individuals and organizations have access to the knowledge and support they need to make a positive difference, contributing to a future where businesses thrive while leaving a meaningful and sustainable impact on society and the world.

Acknowledgments

The creation of "THE VALUE CREATOR: Driving Revenue and Impact in Business" has been a collaborative effort that would not have been possible without the support, dedication, and contributions of many individuals and organizations. We express our heartfelt gratitude to all those who have played a significant role in bringing this book to fruition.

First and foremost, we extend our deepest appreciation to the readers and aspiring value creators whose enthusiasm and passion for driving positive change inspired us to embark on this journey. Your unwavering commitment to making a difference in the world serves as a constant source of motivation.

We extend our gratitude to the experts, thought leaders, and professionals who generously shared their knowledge and insights, enriching the content of this book. Your expertise and guidance have been invaluable in shaping the ideas presented within these pages.

To the real-life value creators and businesses featured in this book, we extend our sincere thanks for allowing us to share your inspiring success stories and testimonials. Your remarkable journeys serve as shining examples of the transformative power of value creation.

A special thank you to our team of editors, designers, and publishing professionals, whose meticulous efforts and creative talents have brought this book to life. Your dedication to excellence and attention to detail have been instrumental in crafting a captivating reading experience.

We also acknowledge the contributions of the organizations and institutions that have supported and sponsored the research and development of this book. Your belief in the importance of driving revenue and impact in business has made this project possible.

Lastly, we extend our deepest gratitude to our families, friends, and loved ones for their unwavering support and encouragement throughout this endeavor. Your belief in us and your understanding of the time and effort invested in this project have been a constant source of strength.

To all those who have played a part, big or small, in the creation of "THE VALUE CREATOR: Driving Revenue and Impact in Business," we extend our heartfelt appreciation. Your collective efforts have contributed to the realization of our vision - to inspire and empower value creators' worldwide, driving positive change and leaving a lasting impact on businesses, communities, and the world.

With gratitude,

Jim Einstein.

About the Author

Jim Einstein is a renowned and accomplished expert in the realm of business, innovation, and sustainability. With a distinguished career spanning decades, Jim Einstein has consistently demonstrated a remarkable ability to drive revenue and impact through value creation. Their visionary leadership, coupled with a deep understanding of global challenges, has positioned them as a trailblazer in the field.

Throughout their journey, Jim Einstein has founded and led successful ventures, mentored aspiring entrepreneurs, and advised multinational corporations on implementing sustainable practices. Their passion for making a positive difference in the world has fueled groundbreaking initiatives that transcend borders and industries.

As an ardent advocate for the power of value creation, Jim Einstein has inspired audiences worldwide through keynote speeches, workshops, and consulting engagements. Their expertise has been sought after by leading organizations, governments, and educational institutions, making them a respected thought leader in their field.

With an unwavering commitment to fostering a culture of innovation and social responsibility, Jim Einstein endeavors to empower individuals and organizations to embrace their inner value creator. Their captivating storytelling and actionable insights resonate with readers, motivating them to take transformative action and contribute to a sustainable and prosperous future.

In "THE VALUE CREATOR: Driving Revenue and Impact in Business," Jim Einstein shares their wealth of knowledge and real-life experiences, igniting a global movement of value creators who are driving positive change and making a lasting impact on businesses, communities, and the world.